China Briefing

The Practical Application of China Business

For further volumes:
http://www.springer.com/series/8839
http://www.asiabriefingmedia.com

Dezan Shira & Associates is a specialist foreign direct investment practice, providing business advisory, tax, accounting, payroll and due diligence services to multinationals investing in China, Hong Kong, India and Vietnam. Established in 1992, the firm is a leading regional practice in Asia with twenty-two offices in four jurisdictions, employing over 170 business advisory and tax professionals.

We also provide useful business information through our media and publishing house, Asia Briefing.

Asia Briefing Ltd.

China's Neighbors

Who is Influencing China and Who China is Influencing in the New Emerging Asia

Third Edition

Springer

DEZAN SHIRA & ASSOCIATES

Asia Briefing Ltd.
132 Nathan Road
Tsim Sha Tsui, Unit 1618
16/F., Miramar Tower
Kowloon
Hong Kong SAR

ISSN 2191-0634 ISSN 2191-0642 (electronic)
ISBN 978-3-642-27614-9 ISBN 978-3-642-27615-6 (eBook)
DOI 10.1007/978-3-642-27615-6
Springer Heidelberg New York Dordrecht London

Library of Congress Control Number: 2012933867

Printed on acid-free paper

Springer is part of Springer Science+Business Media (www.springer.com)

About Asia Briefing's China Business Guides

Thank you for buying this guide. China Briefing's publications are designed to fill a niche in the provision of information about business in China. This book is a timely reminder of the profound changes that an emerging China is having on the rest of Asia. Rather like throwing a pebble into a pond, the ripples that have spread out from the opening up of China are having a knock-on effect on the economies just across its borders.

Here, we introduce the diversity and developments that are taking place in China's neighbors. The articles and materials within have been researched and written in China by those familiar with the issues faced by foreign invested enterprises. To compile this guide, we have engaged the assistance of a respected professional services firm: Dezan Shira & Associates. Without this firm's assistance this book would not have been possible, and we wholeheartedly recommend their services.

Contributors, editors and designers of previous editions of this guide include: Becky Jian, Chris Wei, Chua Siew Joo, Chris Devonshire-Ellis, Joyce Roque, Andy Scott and Nazia Vasi. Contributors to the current edition also include Simon Sheung and Lena Xia. This edition was laid out by Chris Wei and edited by Kaitlin Shung.

At China Briefing, our motto is "the practical application of China business" and we hope that within this volume and our other publications you feel that we have achieved this.

Sincerely,
Asia Briefing

Contents

About China's Neighbors

In the updated version of this book, we revisit China's neighboring countries and take a look at the regional issues that have affected them this year. For investors in China and the region at large, an understanding of the geopolitical, social and economic ties between these countries can certainly support both short and long-term investment strategy.

1 An Introduction to ASEAN

The Association of Southeast Asian Nations (ASEAN) came into existence more than 40 years ago when the ASEAN Declaration was signed on August 8, 1967. Since that time, the organization has continued to grow and command respect in

Asia Briefing Ltd., *China's Neighbors*, China Briefing,
DOI: 10.1007/978-3-642-27615-6_1,

both regional and international circles. The ten members of ASEAN are Indonesia, Malaysia, the Philippines, Singapore, Thailand, Brunei Darussalam, Vietnam, Laos, Myanmar and Cambodia.

ASEAN exists as a means by which to build and strengthen the links between Southeast Asian countries and to aid economic, social and cultural growth. China retains close ties with ASEAN, although it is technically not a member nation.

Most recently, ASEAN has involved itself in the ongoing territorial disputes regarding the South and East China Sea. In 2011, foreign ministers and officials met at the ASEAN Regional Forum in Bali, Indonesia, where this issue was a key topic on the agenda. The South China Sea is home to important global shipping routes as well as valuable oil and gas reserves, which has drawn China, Taiwan, Brunei, Malaysia, the Philippines and Vietnam to the table to try and claim portions of the territory.

2 World Bank Doing Business Report 2011

East Asia and the Pacific, as well as the Central Asian region, showed promising improvements in the World Bank's 2011 Doing Business publication. The writers of the report commented that despite the difficult economic landscape, given the global financial crisis a year earlier, policy makers have shown a commitment to supporting local businesses through promoting favorable regulations.

Singapore retains its top ranking from the previous year, as does Hong Kong in second place. Out of 183 countries surveyed, China's rank slipped from the previous year, falling from 78 in 2010 to 79 in 2011. In the context of countries that we cover in this book, the Kyrgyz Republic ranks the highest coming in at 44 (compared to 47 in 2010) in 2011. Kazakhstan and Mongolia also rank ahead of China at 59 and 73, respectively. India rose in the rankings by one spot, coming in at 134, far behind Pakistan, Nepal and Russia.

Specifically in respect to East Asia and the Pacific region—in addition to Singapore and Hong Kong–Thailand, Malaysia and Taiwan rounded out the top five easiest countries in which to do business.

Major recent changes to business regulations in the region include the implementation of China's new unified tax law, which has been in the process of being phased in over a number of years. Through unifying foreign and domestic enterprise's tax rates, the process of paying corporate income tax has been greatly simplified. Hong Kong also removed the fuel tax on diesel this year and implemented legal reforms to expedite commercial dispute resolution.

Laos implemented a new value added tax, replacing a business turnover tax, while Vietnam streamlined the licensing process to ease the process of attaining permits and appropriate licensing materials.

Kazakhstan ranked as one of the most improved countries in 2009–2010 for doing business. With improvements in areas such as starting a business, dealing with construction permits, protecting investors and cross-border trade, Kazakhstan jumped 15 places in the rankings from 74 to 59.

3 The Shanghai Cooperation Organization

The economic rise of Asia and the increasing importance of Central Asia, in terms of natural resources and security, have strengthened the role of the Shanghai Cooperation Organization (SCO). The SCO was founded on June 15, 2001 in Shanghai by the leaders of China, Russia, Kazakhstan, Kyrgyzstan, Tajikistan, and Uzbekistan, and was originally formed due to growing security concerns in the region. Its role has been extended to support the creation of economic benefits for member countries as well. India, Iran, Mongolia and Pakistan remain observers of the SCO.

SCO member countries have a collective population of 1.5 billion and cover nearly three-fifths of the Eurasian continent. SCO's highest decision-making body is the Heads of State Council, which meets annually to overview and direct SCO activities and goals.

Although the declaration on the establishment of the SCO contained a statement that it is not an alliance directed against other states and regions and it adheres to the principle of openness, many observers believe that one of the original purposes of the SCO was to serve as a counterbalance to NATO and the United States and in particular, to avoid conflicts that would allow the United States to intervene in areas near both Russia and China.

On the economic front, SCO members have agreed to improve the flow of goods in the region while prioritizing joint energy projects in the oil and gas sector, the exploration of new hydrocarbon reserves, and joint use of water resources.

In order to bolster security among member nations, the SCO focuses on eradicating the threats faced from terrorism, separatism, extremism and drug trafficking. As a result, joint military exercises between the member countries play an important part in securing the region.

Cultural cooperation also occurs in the SCO framework, with member countries holding art festivals and culturals exhibitions in each others' countries.

Shanghai Cooperation Organisation website:
www.sectsco.org

Afghanistan

Formal name: Islamic Republic of Afghanistan
Capital city: Kabul

GDP
US$27 billion

Total Imports & Exports
US$1.68 million

World Bank
"Doing Business"Ranking
167of 183

Population
29.83 million

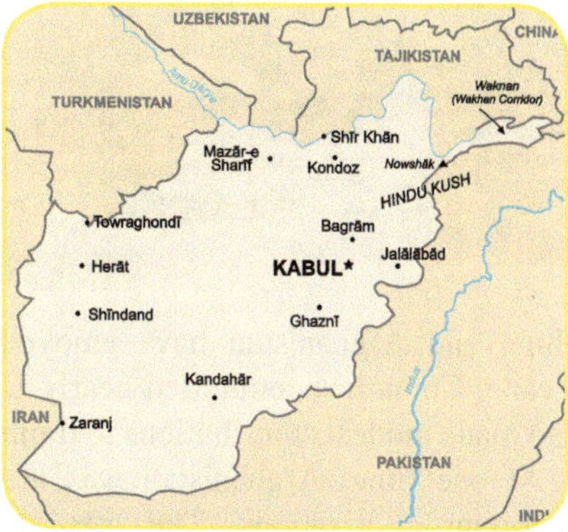

Afghanistan is located along what used to be the ancient Silk Road, and today is in the heart of the Middle Eastern, Central Asian and the Indian subcontinent. The primary languages spoken are Pashtu and Dari, while the local currency is the afghani (AFA) which traded at AFA46.45 to US $1 in 2010. In 2007, Afghanistan became a member of the South Asian Association for Regional Cooperation (SAARC).

Afghanistan has frequented international headlines for its ongoing wars. The Taliban took control of Afghanistan in 1996 and had control of nearly 90% of the country until 2000. Following the 9/11 attacks in New York, the United States entered the country and American initiated attacks allowed opposition parties to prosper. The Taliban were succeeded by Hamid Karzai, who became interim president in 2002 and won the country's first presidential election in 2004.

Afghanistan's economy relies primarily on agriculture, which is estimated to involve 80% of the population. The country also has access to a wealth of mineral resources, in which investment has been limited because of social and political unrest.

Strengthening ties between China and Afghanistan are emerging. In March 2010, President Karzai visited China and signed a number of new agreements in regards to facilitating trade of specific Afghan imports into China. Afghanistan could also, in the future, play an important role in opening trade between China and Central Asia.

Asia Briefing Ltd., *China's Neighbors,* China Briefing,
DOI: 10.1007/978-3-642-27615-6_2, © Asia Briefing Ltd. 2012

1 A Place in Between

China and Afghanistan have enjoyed warmer relations recently. For the last decade, China has committed nearly US $1 billion in aid to Afghanistan and has also made modest contributions to training Afghanistan's National Security Forces.

At one time, Afghanistan was at the center of some of the world's most important civilizations. The arts and sciences thrived, and cultivation and advanced farming techniques turned the plains around Kabul into a great bread basket. In 1219, the Mongols came and left a devastating path of destruction from which the country has never quite recovered from. Since then, Afghanistan has been the setting for "The Great Game" (a tug of war between the British Empire and Russia in the nineteenth century over the area) and also played a prominent role in the collapse of the Soviet Union. Following the 9/11 terrorist attacks in the United States, Afghanistan once again played "host" to world powers.

An Unlucky Country

Ahmad Shah Durrani created the Durrani Empire in 1747, and by 1751, had conquered the entire present day Afghanistan, Pakistan, Khosaran and Kohistan provinces of Iran, along with Delhi in India. Durrani established his capital in Kandahar and his tomb, a pilgrimage site for many, remains there to this day. Following the end of his reign, the country's capital relocated to Kabul in the nineteenth century and much of Afghanistan's territories were ceded to the British. After becoming a buffer state between Britain and Russia, Afghanistan regained full independence from the United Kingdom on August 19, 1919, following the third Anglo-Afghan war.

After relative peace and prosperity in the first half of the twentieth century, Afghanistan has since suffered under a continuous and brutal civil war. In 1978, a Soviet-backed communist coup toppled President Mahommad Daoud and a bloody power-struggle followed. Fighting eventually escalated to a Soviet invasion in December 1979. Following the Soviet pull out in 1989, Afghanistan once again lost any chance for peace as regional factions squared off. With the emergence of the Taliban, war enveloped the country as the Taliban's influence spread and their extreme Islamic policies drew the attention of Western leaders. An American-led invasion eventually toppled the Taliban from power, but failed to bring peace to the country. While NATO troops have assisted the government in gaining control of major urban centers, and billions of dollars have been provided by the international community for reconstruction, the Taliban has proved to be resilient and war continues.

China and Afghanistan

In 2009, China's interests in Afghanistan expanded and extend beyond trade to social stability, which invariably affects China's more remote western regions. The Chinese Ministry of Foreign Affairs reported that the two countries were engaging in high-level talks between President Hu Jintao and President Hamid Karzai in 2010. As well, Chinese investment has played a notable role in infrastructure development through jumpstarting road construction and communication projects.

China has watched the re-emergence of the Taliban with apprehension, given the threat to stability in the region. China's vast frontier province of Xinjiang, inhabited by the Uyghur Muslim minority groups who have traditional ethnic ties to Afghanistan, is a security concern for Beijing. China is interested in helping Afghanistan become a stable, moderate state, that is open to Chinese investment, and perhaps most importantly, free of a Western military presence.

Commercial and Strategic Interests

In 2007, state-owned China Metallurgical Group invested a staggering US $3 billion in Afghanistan's Aynak copper field. The largest foreign direct investment project in the country's history involves not only mining, but also the construction of US $500 million worth of power plants, hospitals, mosques and a railway from Tajikistan to Pakistan to support exploration. The Financial Times reported that that the scope of this project is significant, given that the funds invested would equal more than a third of all international development money spent in Afghanistan between 2002 and 2010.

The investment is only the start of a new Sino-Afghan relationship and is seen by watchers as a test of Afghanistan's feasibility as an investment site. Afghanistan has large unexplored reserves of oil and natural gas in the northern part of the country. Other resources include large iron ore deposits between Heart and the Panjsher Valley and reserves of gold in the provinces of Badakshan, Takhar and Ghazni. As China demands increasing amounts of raw materials for its rapidly expanding economy, these reserves will become strategically important to Beijing.

Border Crossings

There is not currently a viable route between Afghanistan and China, however ancient mountain passes, fit only for donkeys at best, litter the Pamir mountains in this area. The border crossing between the two countries is officially closed. However, this does not prevent Afghani traders from the northern frontier regions from turning up at the regional Sunday commodity market in Kashgar, in western Xinjiang. There have been discussions between the Afghani and Chinese governments concerning the feasibility of developing the Wakhjir Pass into Afghanistan's northern frontier, which if completed would provide access overland to Kabul, through the Pamir mountains across the Hindu Kush from Taxkorgan, where China already has overland port facilities at Khunjerab (currently serving Pakistan). This would provide a direct route from Kabul to Kashgar.

Bhutan

Formal name: Kingdom of Bhutan
Capital city: Thimpu

GDP **US$3.875 billion**	Total Imports & Exports **US$1.129 billion**
World Bank "Doing Business" Ranking **142** of 183	Population **708,427**

Bhutan is a small country nestled between India and China. Formerly isolated, Bhutan opened to foreigners in the 1970s. Bhutan is a member of the South Asian Association for Regional Cooperation (SAARC) and the South Asian Free Trade Agreement (SAFTA). The country is also in the process of joining the WTO. Bhutan's currency is the ngultrum (Nu), which is pegged to the Indian rupee.

Bhutan transitioned into a constitutional monarchy in 2008, electing the country's first Prime Minister, Jigme Thinley. The Bhutanese monarchy has continued to promote "Gross National Happiness" as an important metric, which is indicative of a commitment to economic and spiritual development.

Bhutan's economy is focused in agriculture, which constitutes nearly a third of GDP and which nearly 70% of the population rely on for their livelihood. The country's close ties with India and Bangladesh have had a positive impact on the economy. India remains a key diplomatic and economic partner as Bhutan's largest provider of foreign aid and investment. The country has also focused on hydropower development, which remains an important source of growth and public revenue.

Despite their geographic proximity, China and Bhutan do not share a particularly close partnership although trade between the two countries is on the rise. In 1998, Bhutan and China signed an agreement to "maintain peace and tranquility" along their borders; it is the first and only Sino-Bhutanese peace agreement to date.

Asia Briefing Ltd., *China's Neighbors,* China Briefing,
DOI: 10.1007/978-3-642-27615-6_3,

1 A Changing Country Eyes China with Caution

Bhutan—a land of stunning mountain ranges where mystics and monks have long searched for spiritual enlightenment—remains one of the most mysterious places on Earth. Bhutan is notorious for its resistance to outside influence and a policy of cultural isolation has helped to preserve its traditions and religious teachings.

In 2008, the Kingdom of Bhutan transitioned from an absolute monarchy to a constitutional monarchy, with the constitution being drafted by the king in 2003 and officially adopted by parliament in 2008. In January 2011, the first elections were held for local mayors in Bhutan's four largest cities.

In light of the changes in the political structure, doing business in Bhutan is not what it used to be.

The Happiness Quotient

The Bhutanese government spends an estimated 18% of its budget on providing free education and medical care to all Bhutanese. Bhutan's government has been measuring happiness since 1972 to assess life in the country. Gross national happiness (GNH) is a metric guided by Buddhist spiritual values to enforce policies that would improve the quality of life in holistic and psychological terms.

Despite Bhutan's utopian ideals, the country has not been without violence. In the late 1980s, Tibetan based Bhutanese conflict led to violent ethnic unrest within the country's Nepalese community, which led to an estimated 80,000 Nepalese fleeing to nearby Nepal.

Border Issues

Currently, Bhutan and China do not have formal diplomatic relations. Recently, representatives from both countries have met in response to persistent border disputes. In 2010, the Chinese Assistant Minister of Foreign Affairs, Hu Zhengyue, met with Bhutanese leaders to manage "goodwill and understanding."

For much of its modern history, Bhutan has been closely tied to India, a key trading partner and Bhutan's provider of foreign development aid. By 2020, India has promised to import a minimum of 5,000 MW of electricity from Bhutan. India will also be funding three hydropower projects in the country worth a total of US $1.2 billion, with a combined installed capacity of 1,400 MW.

Bhutan and China

Bhutan shares a 470 km border with China but has four disputed areas that stretch from Doklam towards the ridges from Gamochen and Batangla, Sinchela and down to the Amo Chhu—all in all 269 km^2.

When the Chinese Communist army seized Tibet in 1950, Bhutan was afraid that its sovereignty would be compromised because of Chinese claims to Bhutan as part of Tibet. This led to the closure of the Tibetan–Bhutanese border in the north.

Tense border disputes would put Bhutan on the defensive on what it sees as continuing Chinese advances in its territory. The country's officials seemingly changed position in the 1970s when they supported the "One China" policy and voted for China's seat in the United Nations.

Finally, in 1998 China and Bhutan signed an agreement called the Five Principles of Peaceful Co-existence. The agreement focused on promising peace on the border, as well as China's recognition of Bhutan as a sovereign nation. But by 2002, China would try again to claim ownership of disputed areas. Three years later, Chinese soldiers would be found crossing the border into Bhutan.

Another recent Chinese foray into Bhutan took place in 2007, when the People's Liberation Army started making inroads near the strategic Chumbi Valley, a stretch of land that lies between India, Bhutan and China. The move alarmed Bhutan and India due to the valley's proximity to the often volatile Siliguri Corridor. The region will likely see increased activity by both Chinese and Indian forces in the future as the countries move to secure their strategic interest.

Commercial and Strategic Interests

In December 2010, the Bhutan National Bank and the Asian Development Bank (ADB) signed a trade finance agreement to provide further loans to develop international trade in Bhutan. The EIU predicts the trade deficit in Bhutan will narrow in 2011–2012, as strong levels of grants facilitating construction of new hydropower projects are expected to continue and development aid from foreign nations is expected to drop. The agreement opens the doors for participant banks in Bangladesh, China, India, Nepal, and others in the Asia and Australasia region, to provide financing to small and medium-sized companies in Bhutan.

After granting licenses to two new private banks, T-Bank and Druk Punjab National Bank, the RMA announced in November 2010 that it will hold off on giving any new approvals for 5 years. It will allow the new establishment of branchless banks that use networks of agents to carry out financial services rather than physical branches.

There is also an ongoing dispute regarding the public offering of the Bank of Bhutan, the oldest and largest bank in the country. Established in 1962 in a joint venture between the State Bank of India and the Bhutanese government, the government currently holds 80 percent of the bank. The bank was commanded to go public, and ownership by the government was to be capped at 24% by RMA regulations that required all banks in Bhutan to be public limited companies.

Border Crossings

Bhutan does not have formal diplomatic relations with China, and the border between Bhutan and China is officially closed. Part of this 470 km border area is disputed due to its strategic proximity to the Siliguri intersection where China, Bhutan and India meet. There have been sporadic excursions by Chinese troops into the area, probably to test Indian border defenses, while Bhutan has also complained to China about Tibetan traders raiding forested lands for valuable wild mushrooms and rare herbs.

Bhutan and China do engage in high level discussions on the issue, for example consider the "Bhutan–China Agreement On Maintenance Of Peace And Tranquility Along The Sino-Bhutanese Border Areas, 1998" in which both sides essentially agreed to disagree. There are eleven major mountain passes between Bhutan and Tibet, most at well over 5,000 m, however these officially remain closed to trade or migration and are only accessible in summer months. Part of the Nathu La Pass (see India) has a spur east into Bhutan, this may see development in time.

There are no direct air links between Thimpu and any Chinese cities. Transit usually takes place through Delhi.

Much of Sino-Bhutan trade is, therefore, conducted covertly, with the main trading centers being Lhasa and the Bhutan capital of Thimpu.

India

Formal name: Republic of India
Capital city: New Delhi

GDP
US$4.06 trillion

Total Imports & Exports
US$585.54 billion

World Bank
"Doing Business" Ranking
134 of 183

Population
1.2 billion

India declared independence from colonial rule on August 15, 1947 after being ruled by the British since the early nineteenth century. Pakistan was formed at the same time in recognition of a divide between the Hindu and Muslim majorities. India's currency is the rupee (INR) and the major languages spoken include Hindi and English. India is a republic and part of the British Commonwealth.

India is the world's largest democratic country and also the world's second most populous after China, with a current population of 1.2 billion. Despite only having 2.4% of the world's land area, India's burgeoning and relatively youthful population (the median age is 26.2 years) is likely to bolster the country's economic and diplomatic influence, as it is predicted to outgrow China within the next two decades.

India ranks fifth among the world's largest economies by measure of GDP (purchasing power parity). The Indian economy has averaged 7% annual growth since 1997 and the administration continues to introduce liberal, market-oriented reforms. Among the most promising industries in India is the software industry, which employs a substantial number of the country's well-educated English speakers but the majority of the country continues to rely on agriculture for their livelihood.

China is one of India's key trading partners but India also maintains diplomatic and economic relations with the United States and the Association of Southeast Asian Nations.

Asia Briefing Ltd., *China's Neighbors,* China Briefing,
DOI: 10.1007/978-3-642-27615-6_4, © Asia Briefing Ltd. 2012

1 Rivals and Partners

Between China and India, their combined populations constitute more than a third of total global population. As well, despite similarities in demographics and their mutual emergence as economic powerhouses, it is not clear what the future holds in terms of relations between the two countries.

When it comes to China–India relations, the two Asian behemoths have been playing the great game quite bashfully. They support each other on international fronts, whether it is to arm wrestle rich countries for farm subsidies, hold regular high level diplomatic talks, conduct joint military exercises, fight terrorism or improve air and rail links. However, the two countries often also engage in tug of war—quarreling over land and sea territory, competing for international resources to fuel their rapid growth from Russian, African and Iranian oil, gas and natural resources and often viewing each other with an eye of suspicion.

India arose from the 2008 global financial crisis in better shape than many emerging markets. However, the progress made on cutting the fiscal deficit has nearly all been lost, and the government continues to nurture its growing private sector. Moreover, inflation rose by 8.3% in February and remains a key concern for policy makers.

History

Early Sino-India relations stemmed from trade along the ancient Silk Route, which was the path for the exchange of silks, spices, precious stones and much later the spread of Buddhism between the two countries.

The transmission of Buddhism from India to China has prompted many scholars and monks to travel between the two countries. Indian scholars Batuo, from the

Shaolin Monastery, and Bodhidharna, the founder of Zen Buddhism, traveled to China while Chinese monks and scholars, Xuanzang and I Ching, attended Asia's oldest residential university located in Bihar, India—Nalanda University.

Xuanzang later went on to write an account of his journey to India, which later inspired one of the four great classical novels of Chinese literature, more popularly known in Mandarin as Xi You Ji or "Journey to the West". During that time, China and India exchanged not only Buddhism and goods but also valuable information. For example, Aryabhatta, an Indian astronomer and mathematician, would eventually have his work in trigonometry translated into Mandarin.

During the eighteenth and nineteenth centuries, India's borders were threatened by conflict between Britain and Russia, who were struggling to gain control of the strategically important region. The Russians would eventually continue to press south while the British in India invaded Tibet. The Chinese resisted and were successful in defeating the Sikhs and besieging Leh in Ladakh. At this point, neither side wished to continue the conflict, as the Sikhs were embroiled in tensions with the British that would lead up to the First Anglo-Sikh War, while the Chinese were in the midst of the First Opium War with the British East India Company. Consequently the Chinese and the Sikhs signed a treaty in September 1842, which stipulated no transgressions or interference in each others' frontiers.

Rival Neighbors

For the first half of the twentieth century, although China and India did not interact much, they both concentrated on liberalizing themselves from the shackles of the past and focusing on internal development.

Sino-India relations began to mature in the 1950s, following the formation of the People's Republic of China in 1949 and Indian independence from the British in 1947. The initial bone of contention between the two countries was Tibet. In early 1954, China's Zhou Enlai and India's Jawaharlal Nehru signed the Panchsheel, or the Five Principles of Peaceful Coexistence, which include mutual respect for each other's territorial integrity and sovereignty, mutual non-aggression, mutual non-interference in each other's internal affairs, equality and mutual benefit, and peaceful coexistence.

However, relations quickly soured later that year when China and India both drew official maps and it became clear that both sides were laying claim to territories which the other felt belonged to themselves. Soon, swords were drawn and in 1959, the Dalai Lama fled from Tibet to India. In 1962, the Sino-Indian war commenced. India eventually lost the war and relations with the PRC deteriorated through the rest of the 1960s and the early 1970s. China sided with Pakistan, India's arch rival, and India backed the Soviet Union, China's prime competitor. Consequently, the Nathu La Pass, the main artery through which Chinese and

Indian trade was conducted, was closed which disconnected the two countries politically, culturally and economically.

Strengthening Relationships

While the 1980s began with a mix of diplomatic talks and localized aggression, the wind changed in the 1990s and the two estranged countries sought to recement their historical bonds. Joint talks were held in India and China on the border issue and border trade resumed in July 1992 after a hiatus of more than 30 years. Consulates reopened in Mumbai and Shanghai in December 1992 and June 1993.

In 1993 and 1996, the two sides signed the Sino-Indian Bilateral Peace and Tranquility Accords, an agreement to maintain peace and tranquility along the Line of Actual Control (LoAC). Ten meetings of the Sino-Indian Joint Working Group (SIJWG) and five of an expert group have taken place to determine where the LoAC lies, but little progress has occurred. Recently, both sides have taken steps to recognize the legitimacy of the other as evidenced by China's recognition of the territories of Sikkim and Assam as belonging to India, while India has acknowledged that the Tibet Autonomous Region is part of China.

Through bilateral negotiations, the two countries also signed several agreements on economic, scientific, cultural, technological, media and military cooperation throughout the 1990s.

The twenty-first century saw more progress in Sino-Indian ties. The Nathu La Pass was re-opened, bringing the two countries closer than ever. Today, the economic strengths of both these countries are thus far considered to be somewhat complementary—China is perceived to be strong in manufacturing and infrastructure while India is perceived to be strong in services and information technology.

Present Day

Economic relations between the two countries are escalating. China is one of India's largest trading partners, by measure of total imports and exports. The two countries exchange steel, iron ore, technology, minerals and other raw materials.

As it stands, China maintains an advantage over India in six key areas: scale, integration of value chain, research and development capability, productivity, ease of conducting business, and infrastructure.

In terms of scale, China has maintained and will likely continue to hold onto its significant lead. As of 2009, China exported roughly US $1.4 trillion dollars worth of goods, compared to India's US $200 billion, which means China leads India by a multiple of 7.

However, one must consider that India's economy is only one-third the size of China's. India today is, in many ways, reminiscent of China 30 years ago and consequentially, it has all of the untapped opportunities that go with it. India will continue to rise over the course of this century, much as how China has over the last few decades.

On the cultural front, China and India have held several student, scholar, arts and tourism exchange programs. These programs aim to further bridge the gap between the two nations, helping them better understand each other and work more closely together.

China and India still have a long way to go in understanding each other. The countries may have suffered the same colonial past but the rapid strides China has taken in its path to development ensure that the two countries are not yet politically, culturally or economically aligned. As both countries grow, develop, learn more about each other and continue strong bilateral relations it will benefit not only their dealings, but also that of Asia.

Crossing the land border between India and China is difficult for three reasons. First, much of it is high altitude Himalayan terrain with passes not suitable for modern commercial traffic. Second, the two countries fought a border war in 1962 and a continuing military presence on both sides heavily restricts commercial access, and third, much of the border area is still under dispute and off limits.

Consequently, although diplomatic relations are improving, the only passes are ancient mountain routes and are not really viable other than for local produce—if you can get across at all. There are currently three operational land border crossings for trade and all require special permits to access them from either side. They are not at this moment viable for tourism.

Border Crossings

Sharsingma (India)/Yadong (Tibet)

This is part of the Nathu La Pass, one of the highest mountain passes in the world, which crosses from Sikkim to southern Tibet. It is an ancient trade route with altitude in places over 5,300 m.

The Chinese have been making efforts to make this route and the border area more accessible and the Chinese side possesses decent roads and storage facilities. However, the Indian side remains strictly controlled and with little infrastructure. A daily import/export market for local produce, such as wool, textiles, traditional medicines and low end products, has opened at Yadong and permits local residents visa-free travel between the two countries, but at present this has not been extended to allow crossings for foreigners. However, as part of China's western development strategy, there are plans to extend the Qingzang railway from Lhasa to Yadong, near the Nathu La Pass that marks the China–India border to Yadong.

There are two other notable passes close by this region, notably the Namchi/Kalimpong Pass, closed since 1962, also known as Jelep La, and a similar route which feeds into Tibet from Gangtok, an ancient royal seat for the then independent Kingdom of Sikkim.
These routes, if eventually fully opened, would rehabilitate the Tibetan trading route for goods to be exported via the Indian port of Kolkota, further to the south, and would assist

with the redevelopment of Lhasa and Xigaze as Tibetan trading centers. Gangtok is on the main Indian highway network, while the nearest Indian rail connection is at Shiliguri, about 60 km south of the pass.

Khorzak (India)/Purang (Tibet)

This crossing, also known as the Lipulekh Pass was reopened in 1992, and borders the north Indian state of Utteranchal, the western Nepalese border, and the Tibetan town of Purang.

It has been used since ancient times by traders, mendicants and pilgrims transiting between India and Tibet. Presently it is a border post manned by the Indo-Tibetan border police. Lipulekh is open for cross-border trade every year from June through September.

The items cleared for export from India are jaggery, sugar crystals, tobacco, spices, buckwheat flour, coffee, vegetable oil and various miscellaneous consumable items, whereas the main imports from Tibet are sheep and goats and raw silk.

Daubling (India)/Shipki La (Tibet)

This is another ancient Tibetan trade route, located at the far northwestern Indian state of Himachal Pradesh, and the western Tibetan province of Nagari. It historically provided access into Tibet for Indian produce, and access into the trading town of Shimla and Delhi for Tibetan goods. It was reopened for trade in 1994 and is operated seasonally, from April to mid-October.

India is becoming increasingly well connected via air to China, with regular services between Delhi and Beijing, Shanghai and Mumbai, and Kolkota and Guangzhou. The resident Chinese Tibetan population in Kolkata, long the nearest port city to Lhasa, is the highest in India, and the city has India's largest Chinatown. If routes from southern Tibet permanently reopen and are redeveloped for modern commerce into India, these border areas could boom.

Kazakhstan

Formal name: Republic of Kazakhstan
Capital city: Astana

GDP
US$196.4 billion

Total Imports & Exports
US$90.14 billion

World Bank
"Doing Business" Ranking
59 of 183

Population
15.52 million

Kazakhstan is a physically large country, roughly equivalent in size to all of Western Europe. Kazakhstan declared independence from the Soviet Union in 1991, the last Soviet-controlled nation to do so. An ethnically diverse country, Kazakhs only make up 50% of the population while the remainder is composed of Uzbeks, Koreans, Chechens and other minorities. Kazakhstan's currency is the tenge (KZT) which traded at KTZ147.28 to US $1 in 2010. Major languages spoken include Kazakhand Russian.

The country is a constitutional republic, with much power concentrated in President Nursultan Nazarbayev, who has maintained a stronghold over the country since 1991.

Kazakhstan has substantial mineral resources and is the world's largest producer of uranium. The country has seen significant foreign investment in its oil and gas sector, which are the country's leading economic sector. Major oil fields in production include developments in the Caspian Sea and northwestern Kazakhstan. Kashagan oil field is expected to begin production by 2012–2013, a state-run development in cooperation with a host of other multi-nationals.

Kazakhstan's economy is highly regulated and the government has refocused efforts to diversify its economic portfolio. Key trading partners include China, Germany and Russia and in addition, Kazakhstan has stable relationships with its immediate neighbors. The country is also part of a number of supranational organizations, including the United Nations and the North Atlantic Cooperation Council.

Asia Briefing Ltd., *China's Neighbors,* China Briefing,
DOI: 10.1007/978-3-642-27615-6_5, © Asia Briefing Ltd. 2012

1 Trade and Oil: Central Asia at Stake

The Caspian Sea sits on the borders of five countries: Kazakhstan, Azerbaijan, Turkmenistan, Russia and Iran. Kazakhstan is a major producer of oil, producing 1.54 million barrels per day in 2009. The country's oil output is expected to double within the next decade.

China is currently the world's second largest importer of oil, as well as the world's largest consumer of energy—a title which had previously belonged to the United States for almost a century.

China may not need to look too far to find a solution for its oil needs—the Caspian Sea region and the energy resources available there are in China's backyard. The region may, however, also prove to be contentious, as the United States and the European Union look to grab a stake.

In June 2011, China's President Hu Jintao and Kazakh President Nursultan Nazarbayev met to sign a strategic partnership agreement. China has close ties with Kazakhstan and the two countries plan to "increase trade turnover to US $40 billion" by 2015.

The two countries are also collaborating on completing the Kazkhstan portion of the China-Central Asia natural gas pipeline. As well, they have set up a tax free trade zone along their shared border, called the China–Kazakhstan Korgas International Border Cooperation Center, at an expense of US $2.8 billion. In collaboration with the World Bank and Russia, China is also investing in a highway which will connect Kazakhstan with China and improve transfer of goods between the two countries.

The Ambivalent Partner

Kazakhstan is a country of one million square miles distinctly nestled between two titans—Russia and China—and also shares a border with Uzbekistan, Kyrgyzstan, Turkmenistan and the Caspian Sea. For much of its history, it had struggled to assert its independence from foreign rule. It was only in 1991 that Kazakhstan finally declared independence.

Kazakhstan is literally sitting on a goldmine, with claims that the country possesses the world's tenth largest oil reserves and the world's biggest reserves in lead, tungsten, barite, and uranium. Kazakh oil estimates for 2015 are pegged at 100–110 billion barrels annually. It also has the second biggest reserves of chromite, silver, and zinc, and the third largest of manganese. The country also claims to have significant deposits of gold, copper and iron ore.

Kazakhstan's political clout in Central Asia is becoming increasingly clear and in 2010, Kazakhstan became the first non-European nation to chair the Organization for Security and Cooperation in Europe (OSCE).

While Russia has been cautious in allowing China any access to its Siberian oil deposits or holding any controlling stakes in its oil fields, Kazakhstan has been more willing to cut a deal given the right price. In 2005, the China National Petroleum Company bought the Canadian-run Petrokazakhstan, for US $4.18 billion while spending another US $700 million to have the 962.2-km Atasu-Alashankou pipeline reach the Chinese border.

The Atasu-Alashankou pipeline route has also piqued the interest of Gazprom Neft, the oil arm of Russia's gas giant Gazprom, which delivered 700,000 tons of oil to China via the pipeline in 2009. Other oil companies interested in the route also include Russia's Rosneft and TNK-BP.

On July 11, 2009 the second phase of the Kazakhstan–China pipeline went into operation. Known as the Kenkiyak-Kumkol section, construction began in 2007 and was completed in 2009.

Close ties with China have sparked some concern among Kazakhs, who see China's major investment in the country's infrastructure and energy resources as encroaching on the country's independence.

"Before our eyes a lot of work is being carried out [for China] to acquire a number of oil companies working in Kazakhstan," said deputy Valery Kotovich in a speech, according to The New Europe.

"I have figures that say that if it buys these companies, China will control about 28% of production in the country. If a deal that is currently being carried out with Mangistaumunaigaz is closed, this indicator will exceed 40% of production in Kazakhstan" he said.

Rebuilding a Legend

Another important factor that will foster China's closer ties with Kazakhstan, and its other Central Asian neighbors, is the rebuilding of the legendary Silk Road. In 2010, Kazakhstan began to rebuild the largest portion of the famous trade route. The US $5.68 billion project will be the modern day version of the famous route that once linked Europe with Asia for trade.

The strategy is to stimulate trade by land through the establishment of six new transport corridors, including road links, airports, railway lines and seaports. It will snake through China, Russia, South Asia and the Middle East. Funds for constructing the network will come from aid from multilateral organizations and the countries themselves. The eight countries included in the plan are Afghanistan, Azerbaijan, China, Kazakhstan, Kyrgyzstan, Mongolia, Tajikistan and Uzbekistan.

Other Considerations

Kazakhstan's ties with Russia run deep, both historically and economically. Most of the oil pumped from Kazakhstani fields is directed into pipelines bound for Russia. Looking forward, the government seeks to diversify its direct connections to neighboring countries and gain better leverage in price negotiations with Russia. Limited access to major seas and waterways has also weighed on the government's ability to take more advantage of the country's rich natural resource supply.

Border Crossings

Panfilov (Kazakhstan)/Korgas (China)
Korgas is the largest highway border crossing in China's western regions, and is situated on the Chinese side, 90 km from Yining and 670 km from Urumqi. On the Kazak side, it is 35 km from Panfilov and 378 km from Almaty. Korgas sees nearly three million people and two million tons of goods pass through each year and is a major artery between China and Central Asia. Bus services also operate along this route.

Maganshy (Kazakhstan)/Baktu (China)
Baktu is open year round and connects the Kazak city of Maganshy (60 km) with the Chinese city of Tacheng (17 km). It is 700 km from the former Kazak capital city of Semey Oblast and 621 km from Urumqi.

Baktu is capable of handling 200,000 tons of cargo and 100,000 passengers. A 3,040-square-meter multifunctional inspection hall has been set up, together with four goods yards, each with a storage capacity of more than one million tons. An international passenger bus from Tacheng to Ayaguz and Ust-Kamenogorsk of Kazakhstan runs on a regular basis.

Zaisan (Kazakhstan)/Jimnay (China)
Jimnay is a year round highway crossing and links the Kazak city of Zaisan (60 km) with the Chinese city of Jimnay (24 km). It is also an increasingly popular overland route between Altay (198 km) and Urumqi (650 km). The crossing is currently being upgraded and can accommodate traffic of 50,000 people and 100,000 tons of goods.

Dostyk (Kazakhstan)/Alashankou (China)
This crossing, also known as the Alataw Pass, is the main rail crossing between the two countries, and also has significant highway routes, all mainly serving traffic between Almaty and Urumqi. It is China's second largest land port of entry and accommodates more than 90% of all imports and exports into Xinjiang.

Other seasonal border crossings between Kazakhstan and China exist at Aheytubiek, Dulart and Mulart. Themain bilateral trading markets in Kazakhstan and China are in Almaty and Urumqi.

There are regular flights from Astana (capital city), and Almaty to Urumqi.

Kyrgyzstan

Formal name: Kyrgyz Republic
Capital city: Bishkek

GDP
US$12.02 billion

Total Imports & Exports
US$5.71 million

World Bank "Doing Business" Ranking
44 of 183

Population
5.59 million

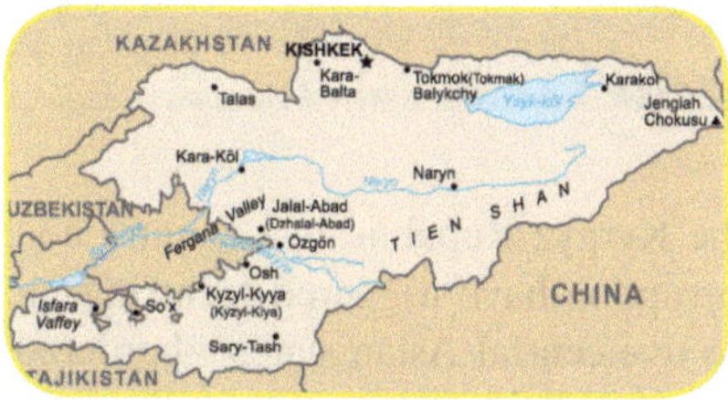

Kyrgyzstan is located in Central Asia, bordered to the east by China and north by Kazakhstan. With access to some oil and gas resources, Kyrgyzstan has economic potential but social unrest and political instability have plagued this former Soviet country. The local currency is the som (KGS), which traded at KGS46.337 to US $1 in 2010. Primarily languages spoken include Kyrgyz and Russian.

The country is a republic, currently managed under the leadership of former Foreign Minister Roza Otunbayeva, following the ousting of President Kurmanbek Bakiyev in April 2010. Bakiyev was named president in 2005 but failed to maintain peace and stability within the country. The next elections are scheduled for October 2011.

Kyrgyzstan's economy has struggled since declaring independence from Soviet rule in 1991, but governmental actions indicate that they continue to aspire towards becoming a free market economy. Agriculture plays an important role in Kyrgyzstan's economy and primary trading partners include Russia, China and Kazakhstan.

The Economist Intelligence Unit reported that the country's difficulties with revenue-raising, coupled with high social spending, led to a substantial budget deficit in 2011–2012. Furthermore, GDP contracted by 1.4% in 2010.

In May 2011, the IMF agreed to extend a borrowing agreement with the Kyrgyz Republic totaling US $106 million. The IMF has also reported that core inflation has stabilized and deflation was recorded in May of 2011.

Asia Briefing Ltd., *China's Neighbors*, China Briefing,
DOI: 10.1007/978-3-642-27615-6_6, © Asia Briefing Ltd. 2012

1 A Leadership Role in Central Asia

The Kyrgyz Republic is a country continually on uneven footing, as poverty and corruption have triggered recurring violence. It is the second smallest country of the five central Asian states—bordered by Kazakhstan to the north, Uzbekistan to the west, Tajikistan to the southwest and China to the east. Despite being a land blessed with breathtaking natural beauty—some calling its Tien Shan range "the Switzerland of Central Asia"—it is one of the poorest countries in the world with an estimated one-third of its population living below the poverty line.

The Tulip Revolution

In 1991, under the leadership of Askar Akayev, the country declared independence from the former Soviet Union. Separation from the Kremlin would lead to devastating effects for the local economy, as an estimated 98% of exports went to the Soviet Union and this hindered the country's free market ambitions.

Akayev was ousted in 2005, during a popular revolt called the "Tulip Revolution." Accusations flew that the government had interfered with parliamentary elections and tensions were aggravated by widespread poverty and corruption.

Russian-educated Kurmanbek Bakiyev was elected in July 2005. The next 3 years were characterized by a volatile political environment, which deterred foreign investment. Issues like privatization of state owned enterprises, expansion of democracy and political freedoms, inter-ethnic relations and terrorism remain unresolved.

Bakiyev himself would be booted from office in April 2010 during a popular uprising and Roza Otunbayeva, Kyrgyzstan's former foreign minister, would be appointed interim president until the next elections.

In Search of Gold

Kyrgyztan's major cash cow is gold, with 40% of industrial output and 60% of exports coming from gold mining. The country also has deposits of coal, gold, uranium, antimony and other rare-earth metals. Outside the gold mining industry, its economy is ill-equipped and a snapshot of domestic commerce shows that the majority of trade is unregulated in small village kiosks and bazaars.

The Kyrgyzaltyn Joint Stock Company was formed in 1992, as a state enterprise to manage Kyrgyzstan's mining industry. In combination with its partners, Kyrgyzaltyn JSC mines nearly 97% of gold unearthed in the country.

Partnerships

Kyrgyzstan is a member of the Shanghai Cooperation Organization (SCO). In 2011, military chiefs of the SCO met to improve military relations and collaborate on collective defense and security. In addition, they also agreed to improve cooperation to combat cross-border crimes and other non-traditional security threats. Kyrgyzstan's deputy defense minister and chief of staff of Armed Forces committed to strengthening military relations between Kyrgyzstan and China.

Another factor that will enhance bilateral relations is the completion of the highway corridor that will connect China, Kyrgyzstan, and Uzbekistan. China has invested US $660 million and plans to finish its section of the corridor by September 2013.

The corridor is being financed under the framework of the Central Asia Regional Economic Cooperation (CAREC), which has garnered support from agencies such as the Asian Development Bank (ADB).

In June of 2011, it was announced that the Asian Development Bank would be providing a US $55 million loan to help finance a 37-mile long high way between Bishkek, Kyrgyzstan and Kashi, China. A statement from the ADB recognized this undertaking as a "must-do project" and will be completed as part of the CAREC Program. In its entirety, CAREC consists of six trade corridors interlinking Central Asian countries.

Playing the Geopolitical Game

China and Kyrgyzstan have maintained diplomatic relations in the past 15 years. The Sino-Kyrgyz Friendly Treaty on Good-Neighborly Cooperation, signed in 2002, further developed economic relations. In August 2010, China and Kyrgyzstan signed an agreement covering bilateral relations and committed to anti terrorism efforts, military cooperation and trade. The treaty also placed particular emphasis on national sovereignty and territorial integrity.

More than the issue of trade, Kyrgyzstan relations seem to be at the bedrock of China's Central Asia diplomatic strategy. China is stockpiling Kyrgyz goodwill because Kyrgyzstan is at the center of the Central Asian region. Ultimately, whoever exerts the most influence on the country will already have gained a gateway for intelligence activities and military operations in sensitive areas like Afghanistan, Pakistan, China and even Russia.

Already, Kyrgyzstan plays host to several foreign military bases: the Russians at Kant Airbase and the Americans at Manas Air Base. If the cards are dealt right, Central Asia could become an integration zone for security and economic affairs that will reconceptualize world regions with China at its helm.

Border Crossings

Artux (Kyrgyzstan)/Kashgar (China)

Known as the Topa, or Torugart Port, this crossing lies at an elevation of 2,000 m, and connects the Kyrgyzcity of Artux (62 km) and Kashgar (57 km).It is a major artery for overland traders using the Kashgar market, Central Asia's largest trading hub, and a regular bus service exists between Bishkek, the capital of Kyrgyztsan, through Artux and onto Kashgar.

The crossing originally used to be located at Torugart (which still remains a border crossing), some 120 km to the south, but the location was found to be unsuitable for most cross border trade and was moved to Topa in 1995. A highway however still connects Topa with the original Torugart Pass. Topa is now a class A international port and handles about 60,000 passengers, 20,000 vehicles and 250,000 tons of cargo annually. Other seasonal ports exist at Year keshtan and Biedieli.

There are evaluation studies currently being conducted to assess the feasibility of extending the current China rail network, which terminates at it's western-most point at Kashgar, to Bishkek, the capital of Kyrgyzstan.

There are regular flights from Bishkek and Osh to Urumqi.

Laos

Formal name: Lao People's Democratic Republic
Capital city: Vientiane

GDP
US$15.69 billion

Total Imports & Exports
US$4.21 billion

World Bank
"Doing Business" Ranking
171 of 183

Population
6.48 million

Laos is one of the few remaining communist states in the world and since 2005, the country has been implementing economic reforms to gradually liberalize its economy. It is a landlocked country and 75% of employment comes from subsistence agriculture. Laos' currency is the Lao PDR kip (LAK) and it has a floating exchange rate. The official language in Laos is Laotian.

Laos has also achieved progress in reducing child mortality, according to the United Nations Children's Fund. It is on target to reach the U.N. Millennium Development Goal of reducing the under-five child mortality rate by two-thirds by 2015.

China has been pouring aid and investment into Laos since 2000. In 2010, China overtook Thailand as the largest foreign investor in Laos. With greater infrastructure development in the Greater Mekong Sub-Region, the number of Chinese living and working in Laos has also been increasing steadily.

Besides being connected by economic migration, Laos and China have recently pledged to strengthen ties through the conservation and management of natural resources. A general agreement has been reached and a forum for the sharing of technical knowledge has been established. As the years progress, both countries are continually extending their cooperation in social, political and economic matters.

Asia Briefing Ltd., *China's Neighbors*, China Briefing,
DOI: 10.1007/978-3-642-27615-6_7, © Asia Briefing Ltd. 2012

1 Southeast Asia's Poorest Gain Access to Consumer Goods

The Lao People's Democratic Republic is a single-party socialist republic nestled in a land-locked section of Southeast Asia. The country shares its borders with Vietnam to the east, Thailand to the west, Cambodia to the south, and China and Myanmar to the north. The capital city is Vientiane, and other major cities include Luang Prabang, Savannakhet and Pakse. It is a member of both the Asia Pacific Trade Agreement (APTA) and the Association of Southeast Asian Nations (ASEAN). Laos applied to join the World Trade Organization (WTO) in July 1997 and its potential membership is still under examination by the international community.

From kingdom to Republic

The earliest recorded history of a unified state in Laos was the Kingdom of Lan Xang in 1353. Literally meaning the "Kingdom of a Million Elephants," Lan Xang was a mighty state revered for its large army of war elephants.

As one of the wealthiest and most powerful kingdoms in the region, Lan Xang extended many of its ideals to the rest of Southeast Asia. For example, in the sixteenth century King Setthathirat helped to spread Buddhism as the predominant religion in the area. Today, around 65% of the population in Laos still practices the religion.

The kingdom flourished for many years but Lan Xang began to see its decline in the late seventeenth century. During this time, the state was plagued with infighting between warring dynasties and violent conflicts with neighboring countries. By 1707, the country split into three kingdoms: Luang Prabang, Vientiane and Champasak, all of which paid tribute to rulers in Siam.

In the latter half of the nineteenth century, France began the colonization of Vietnam. Gradually, the French replaced Siam as the dominant power in Southeast Asia, and brought the three kingdoms of the Lao people into its empire. The Franco-Siamese treaty signed in 1907 outlined the boundary between Laos and Thailand, which still stands today.

After the end of the Second World War, there was a period of intense nationalism among the people of Laos, leading them to declare independence in 1945. However, this was short-lived when France sent colonial troops in the following year to consolidate its hold over the nation. By this time, the Communist movement had spread to Southeast Asia, and the conflict in ideology eventually led to the French-Indochina War between France and the Communist forces from Southeast Asia.

After years of fighting, French forces eventually withdrew from the region, and Laos was granted full sovereignty as part of the Geneva Peace Conference in 1954. Communist revolutionaries eventually consolidated their hold and the Lao People's Democratic Republic was established in 1975.

From then on, the new Communist government established a command economy along with strict security measures. This included total control of the media and the establishment of "re-education camps," institutions which jailed many supporters and dissidents from the previous government. These policies eventually led to hard oppression and economic decline, causing many Laotians to flee the country.

It is estimated that since 1975, approximately 30,000 Laotians claimed refugee status and settled in Western countries such as the United States, France, Canada and Australia, while more than 40,000 fled to neighboring Thailand. The exodus of the Laotian people continued until the late-1990s, when the Lao government gradually eased its policies, closing many of its camps and releasing its prisoners.

While Laos retains its Communist leadership today, it has begun to foster a free market economy and to relax its control on media and security. Despite its agrarian economy and dependence on foreign aid, Laos has enjoyed a long period of economic growth, and is now working with the international community to improve its social and economic development.

A Home to a New Migrant Class

One of the most prominent characteristics of Sino-Laotian relations is the contemporary influx of Chinese migrants to the Southeast Asian country. While nationalism has hindered many of Chinese descent in countries like Malaysia and Indonesia from taking office, they long ago became the de facto merchants and bankers of the region.

This was no exception in Laos, as large groups of Chinese have been migrating to the country since the early 1800s. Today, a new wave of Chinese immigrants is flooding south. Far from the rich and powerful families that preceded them, these

Chinese come from the country's interior, a location that has missed much of the economic transformation of China's eastern coast.

The Road South

In addition to providing extensive support for general aid and development projects, China has a strong trading partnership with Laos. With no access to the sea, Laos depends on its neighbors to acquire shipped goods, and thus has an extensive transportation network. To the north, China and Laos are connected at the border by their respective cities of Mohan and Boten.

Once trucks and busses have passed through the border post at Boten, Laos, they continue south on Highway 1 towards Oudomxai province, the most important crossroads in Northern Laos which links routes to and from Thailand, Vietnam and China. The province's capital, Muang Xai, serves as the junction of Highways 1, 2 and 4. The city represents the heart of the China-Laos trade route, and is home to many small businesses run by Chinese interests.

Further south, Highway 1 meets up with Highway 13, the great artery of Laos, running the entire length of the country. Because it runs through Vientiane, this highway is one of the two main corridors for trade between China and Thailand (the other running by way of Oudomxai through Chiang Khong in Northern Thai province of Chiang Rai).

Goods flowing across the border from China to Laos are often transported on private bus lines, and the relative size of the customs house in Boten reflects the Laotian government's problems with regulating imports and exports. Trucks bound for China are constantly pulling out of the Customs parking lot carrying Laos' natural resources for the growing economic giant. On their way across the border, they pass trucks and busses heading south with cheap Chinese consumer products, goods that a few years ago only the richest in Laos could afford.

An Emerging Free Market

The extent of China's influence on the Laotian economy is evident when one observes the influx of Chinese goods in Laos. On August 2007, the Sanjiang Shopping Mall, a large shopping center specializing in Chinese goods opened in Laos' capital. The mall currently covers 174,000 square meters with over 300 individual shop spaces. Of those, over 200 have been filled by Chinese merchants with the remaining 100 or so spaces being filled by Lao businesses. Built at the cost of US $6 million, the shopping mall is part of a larger US $18 million investment project by the Sanjiang Company, a Chinese investment firm. Unlike the older Morning Market, which contains Lao handicrafts and Thai consumer products, approximately 80% of the goods sold at the Chinese market are imported from China.

Whether it is small electronics, appliances, or one of the thousands of 100-cc. motorcycles that crowd the streets of Vientiane, Chinese goods are becoming more affordable, and changing the face of Laos.

A Rising Powerhouse

In addition to the sale of retail goods, public works projects are also prominent in Laos' economic development, and are currently among the government's primary focuses. The country's location would allow it to supply energy to neighboring fast developing economies, like Thailand and Vietnam. According to the Laotian government, the country has the potential to produce up to 28,000 MW of hydropower from the Mekong River and the 16 Mekong tributaries.

The development of hydroelectric power is still relatively new in Laos, and was sparked by the recent construction of the Nam Theun 2 Hydroelectric Dam. The dam was built on the Nam Theun River, and went into operation in early 2010. It is capable of generating 1,070-MW of electricity, 95% of which is exported to Thailand. The remaining 5% will be reserved for domestic usage. The project is expected to generate US $2 billion in revenue over a 25-year period, much of which will be used to help fund the Laotian government's National Growth and Poverty Eradication Strategy.

Border Crossings

Boten (Laos)/Mohan (China)

This is currently the only significant trade crossing along the 700 km China-Laos border. Trade activity has greatly improved since Laos, Thailand and Vietnam signed the GMS Cross-Border Transport Agreement in 1999. These plans, which were mediated by the Asian Development Bank, facilitated the construction of the Kunming-Bangkok Expressway, which passes through the Boten-Mohan border and carries an estimated US $400 billion worth of goods annually.

By air, Laos is directly connected to China via Kunming.

Myanmar

Formal name: Union of Myanmar
Capital city: Naypyidaw

GDP
US$76.47 billion

Total Imports & Exports
US$17.06 billion

World Bank
"Doing Business" Ranking
N/A

Population
54 million

Myanmar has long been ruled by a military junta. The largest ethnic group in Myanmar is the Bamar, also known as the Burman people. They constitute over 60% of the total population and their dominance has often fuelled intermittent separatist rebellions within the country. The official language in Myanmar is Burmese, and its currency is the kyat (K). Its average exchange rate in 2010 was 966 kyats per US $1.

Myanmar's political structure had undergone a large scale restructuring since the controversial national election in November 2010. The military-backed Union Solidarity and Development Party received 80% of the seats in Myanmar's parliament, and the former Prime Minister Thein Sein was elevated to the role of President. Despite reform, many allege that the new government is still under control of the military's top brass, who have refused to transfer political power to Aung San Suu Kyi's National League for Democracy, which won the last democratically held election in 1990.

Myanmar's economy has seen steady growth in recent years, with growth of 5.3% in 2010. Due to recent discoveries of oil and natural gas, along with new investment in industry, Myanmar's FDI increased from US $329.6 million in 2009–2010 to over US $20 billion in the 2010–2011 economic year.

While the energy sector is expanding rapidly, agricultural production is still the dominant industry and currently makes up about 43% of the country's economy. Principal crops are rice, beans and pulses, sugarcane and culinary crops.

Asia Briefing Ltd., *China's Neighbors,* China Briefing,
DOI: 10.1007/978-3-642-27615-6_8, © Asia Briefing Ltd. 2012

1 China's Burmese Days

Much of Myanmar's ancient monuments, cities, jungles, snow-capped mountains and beaches have remained unexplored. It is a country rich in natural resources, notably petroleum, timber, minerals, precious stones and natural gas but remains relatively poor due to the mismanagement of these resources.

Contemporary Myanmar

Myanmar stands in stark contrast to other developing economies in the Southeast Asian region. While it is a state still deep in political transition, the country struggles with corruption and political oppression. Once a British colony, Myanmar declared independence in 1948, and from 1962 to 2011, the country has been under official control of the military junta, a group comprised of the country's top military officials.

In 1989, the government changed the country's name from Burma to Myanmar and its capital from Rangoon to Yangon. The change in name has garnered controversy in international circles, with some countries having acknowledged the change, while others, such as the United States and its Western allies, have refused to accept it in defiance of the oppressive government.

The first multi-party elections in Myanmar were held in 1990, and led to a majority win by the National League of Democracy, headed by Aung San Suu Kyi. The military junta refused to honor the results of the elections and instead imprisoned Suu Kyi. In the following years, Suu Kyi would be known across the world as a champion for pro-democracy and human rights, and was awarded the Nobel Peace Prize in 1991. Throughout the 1990s and early-2000s, she was released and arrested several times, but after her convoy was attacked by a government-sponsored mob while touring northern Myanmar in 2003, she was placed under house arrest on stricter terms and intermittently placed in the infamous Insein prison. Suu Kyi was finally released from house arrest on November 13, 2010, less than a week after Myanmar's national elections. In total, Aung San Suu Kyi had been imprisoned for over 15 years.

The junta garnered further controversy in 2005 when they unexpectedly relocated their capital from Yangon to Naypyidaw, a remote and undeveloped city 390 km to the north. Chinese diplomats were not immediately notified of the move, and criticized the act at the time. "To set up a thriving city with complete facilities and infrastructure in this patch of land without a single foundation," the embassy in Yangon once said, "will doubtless be a serious test for the government."

In November 2006, the International Labour Organization charged the military junta with subjecting its citizens to forced labor. In the past, there have been reports of thousands of civilians killed or imprisoned to clamp down on those opposing the government. In September 2007, a major crackdown ensued in response to civilian protests against the government. Although these incidents were denied by the majority of Myanmar's officials, there have been eyewitness accounts of thousands of civilians tortured and executed by armed forces.

The most recent incident to incite global outcry has been Myanmar's reaction following the arrival of Cyclone Nargisa in 2008. In the critical days following the disaster, the junta refused international aid despite being ill-equipped to handle the catastrophe. They relented only after weeks of international pressure. The aftermath of Cyclone Nargis led to an estimated 138,000 fatalities.

Until March 2011, the country was directly ruled by the military administered State Peace and Development Council (SPDC). The SPDC, composed of the nation's top 12 military generals, controlled all aspects of life in the country. The council officially dissolved when it transferred power over to the newly-elected parliament, led by the pro-military Union Solidarity and Development Party, which won the national election in November 2010. However, many critics have interpreted this as a thinly-guised attempt by the military to stay in power, and have stated that real power still lies in the hands of General Than Shwe, who has ruled Myanmar for the last 20 years.

Battle for the Indian Ocean

The country has long been under international pressure to invoke government reform. Thus far, the United States and European Union are at the forefront of this effort, and have enacted economic sanctions that forbid most Western companies from investing in Myanmar.

Notably absent from Myanmar's list of detractors are India and China. Both countries have chosen to remain relatively silent and engage the ruling junta, while not publicly supporting their rule. As such, they have often been criticized as being too lenient on the military regime. China has been supplying the Burmese with arms and military training for years while India has actively sought contracts for Myanmar's rich energy sources, as well as agreements to establish transport corridors that will connect it to the country.

Myanmar has a deep relationship with China, given the similarities between the languages, as well Chinese immigrants have long settled in Myanmar as merchants and traders.

Today, both China and India vie for Myanmar's agreement to house the countries' naval forces. The country that outmaneuvers the other will enjoy the strategic advantage of having access to the northeastern part of the Indian Ocean.

Border Crossings

Muse (Myanmar)/Ruili (China)

This is the main border crossing between the two countries and is part of the old Burma Road, built by the Allied Forces during World War II to get supplies from India and Burma to Chinese and Allied troops fighting the Japanese. Muse lies 400 km east of Mandalay, while Ruili is 100 km west of Dali and 450 km northwest from Kunming. Ruili is connected by air to Kunming.

This crossing is to be significantly developed as per a 2008 agreement between the two countries. Myanmar has created a 150 ha trade zone on its side, while the Chinese city of Ruili has long been an old trading center. Ruili alone accounts for 70% of Yunnan province's border trade with neighboring countries.

Narcotics smuggling and human trafficking remain a security concern along the Myanmar–Chinese border, although it is anticipated the ongoing encouragement of legitimate trade will decrease economic dependence on these over time. Genuine bilateral trade has been significantly increasing since these two countries developed stronger trade and economic links. Bilateral trade amounted to US $4.4 billion in 2010, a 53.2% increase from the previous year. At the border alone, Myanmar's export to China was approximately US $567 million, while its import from the latter was at US $486 million.

The border is also the site of the Myanmar–China Border Trade Fair, an annual business expo that alternates between each country's border towns. The latest fair was held in Muse, Myanmar in April 2011.

Myanmar has four other border crossings with China at Lwejei, Laizar, Chinshwehaw and Kambaiti, however the Muse-Ruili crossing is by far the largest and most developed. There are regular flights from Yangon and Mandalay to Kunming, and as of March 2011, there are direct flights from Yangon to Guangzhou.

Narcotic smuggling and human trafficking remain a security concern along the Myanmar-Chinese border, although it is anticipated the ongoing encouragement of legitimate trade will decrease economic dependence on these over time. Genuine bilateral trade has been significantly increasing since these two countries developed stronger trade and economic links. Bilateral trade amounted to US$4.4 billion in 2010, a 53.2% increase from the previous year. At the border alone, Myanmar's export to China was approximately US$567 million, while its import from the latter was at US$480 million.

The border is also the site of the Myanmar-China Border Trade Fair, an annual business expo that alternates between each country's border towns. The latest one was held in Muse, Myanmar in April 2011.

Myanmar has four other border crossings with China at Lweje, Laiza, Chinshwehaw and Kambaiti, however the Muse-Ruili crossing is by far the largest and more developed. There are regular flights from Yangon and Mandalay to Kunming, and as of March 2011 there are direct flights from Yangon to Guangzhou.

Mongolia

Formal name: Mongolia
Capital city: Ulaan Baatar

GDP
US$11.02 billion

Total Imports & Exports
US$6.88 billion

World Bank
"Doing Business" Ranking
73 of 183

Population
3.13 million

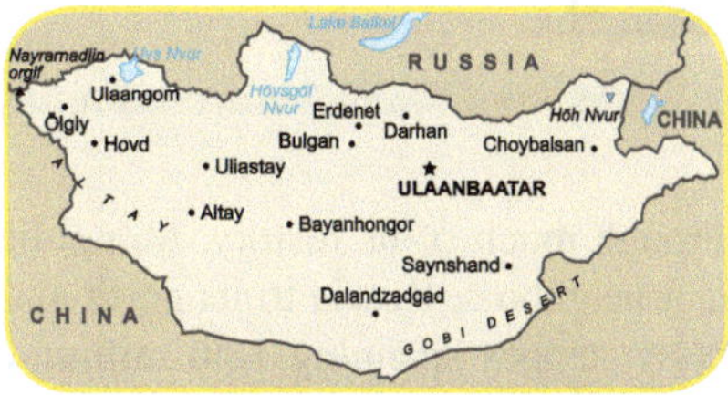

Mongolia was once the center of an empire which stretched from Vienna to the South China Sea. Having a distinct language and unique culture, Mongolia declared independence from China after the fall of the Qing Dynasty in 1911, but soon after fell under Soviet influence. After the breakup of the Soviet Union in 1990 and the subsequent withdrawal of much-needed Soviet support, the Mongolian economy collapsed, triggering poverty and unemployment. Since then, Mongolia has worked to hasten economic recovery. The official currency in Mongolia is the togrog (MNT) and its average exchange rate in 2010 was MNT1357.50 to US $1.

As a parliamentary republic, Mongolia's government is headed by a Prime Minister and President, who acts as Chief of State. Since 2009, these roles have been filled by Prime Minister Sukhbaatar Batbold and President Tsakhia Elbegdorj. Among the government's top priorities in recent times is to bolster national socioeconomic development, a task which they are seeking to complete through international cooperation and resource contracting. While the economy shrunk by 1.3% in 2009 due to the global financial crisis, it has since recovered thanks to 6.5% growth in export of natural resources in 2010.

Mining is continuing to rise as a major industry in Mongolia. By 2016, the government is hoping to raise at least US $25 billion by contracting the mining of its resources to international companies.

Asia Briefing Ltd., *China's Neighbors*, China Briefing,
DOI: 10.1007/978-3-642-27615-6_9, © Asia Briefing Ltd. 2012

1 Eyeing the Vast Resources of a Northern Neighbor

Through much of its history, Mongolia had been subject to the whims of its two giant neighbors, Russia to its north and China to the south. It is a country of vast, grassy steppes spanning 1.56 million square kilometers. Mongolia was home to Genghis Khan, the great Mongol warrior who unified the country's many tribes and conquered much of Asia in the twelfth century. The Mongolian Empire reached as far west as Hungary but following the death of Kublai Khan, Mongolia went into sharp decline and China and Russia began to reassert their influence over the land-locked country. China successfully invaded Mongolia during the Ming Dynasty and following World War II, Mongolia became a satellite state to the Soviet Union and was subject to many of its communist policies.

Today, Mongolia's neighbors are again playing a vital role in the present and future of the country. China was the country's top trading partner in 2010, accounting for 61.7% of its total trade activity. Russia followed second with 13.7%.

In light of China's economic hold on Mongolia, it is no surprise that it is drifting more towards the company of its eastern neighbor. Mongolia has already made plans to join organizations where China is also a member and in turn, China has said that it will support the country's bid to be a part of the Asia–Pacific Economic Community (APEC) and the Asia-Europe Meeting (ASEM). For the moment, Mongolia enjoys observer status as part of the Shanghai Cooperation Organization (SCO).

Mining the Cash Cow

Mongolia is a miner's dream come true. The country boasts of 680 major mineral deposit sites that contain stores of coal, copper, gold, silver, iron, wolfram, molybdenum and fluorspar, to name a few. These minerals, bases and precious metals are necessary for the production of everything from energy to construction to mobile phones and transportation.

Mining contracts have been pouring into its capital, Ulaan Bataar, with such enthusiasm that many have nicknamed the country as Asia's "El Dorado"—the legendary city of gold.

Coal takes the top spot as Mongolia's key export. In the first quarter of 2011, coal made up 33% of total export production, while copper followed with 28.5%. The Mongolian market for coal has grown in the last few years due to increased demand from an energy-hungry China. Mongolia's volume of exported coal in 2010 was 16.6 million tons, 7.1 million tons in 2009, 4.2 million tons in 2008 and only 3.3 million tons in 2007.

Tavan Tolgoi is a mining network in the Gobi Desert, and is the world's largest undeveloped coking coal deposit. It has recently been attracting suitors interested in winning its licensing rights. The mine is estimated to be capable of yielding 6.4 billion metric tons of thermal and coking coal. Tavan Tolgoi is also a point of contention in Mongolian politics because the government has been brokering the rights to mine in the area.

Although copper was recently overtaken by coal as Mongolia's top export, it remains a key part of the country's economic production. Copper is used extensively in the construction industry through wiring, roofs, heating systems, finishings, gas and water tubings. A typical house today would need around 200 kg of copper alone to outfit it with bathrooms and appliances.

Molybdenum, a byproduct of copper mining and another major export, is mainly used as an alloy for stainless steel, cast iron, and super alloys for infrastructure building. China is one of the primary producers of molybdenum, but recent government decisions have led the country to classify the metal as a "national mining resource" and they have consequentially imposed numerous quotas and export duty taxes on the resource. This had the side effect of raising the nation's demand, and generating the need to import more supplies.

As for copper, China's mammoth needs are in stride with its rapid industrialization. It was estimated that the country consumed up to 40% of world copper supplies in 2010, and its consumption rate is expected to be higher in the coming years, albeit at a slower rate.

Development Through Dependent Ties

China's heavy demand for Mongolia's resources has given the country steady economic growth of around 7% annually from 2005 to 2008. While the economy shrunk by 1.7% in 2009 due to the global financial crisis, Mongolia has since rebounded and is expected to have near 10% growth in 2011. The country's destiny seems to be trapped by its land-locked and isolating geographic position that leaves it no choice but to make the best of its dependence on China. Unless Mongolia works to diversify away from its reliance on its mineral wealth, it will continue to depend largely on foreign investment to drive its growth.

Although Mongolia has no problem attracting business ventures, the country still lacks the necessary framework to accommodate them. This is mainly due to poor infrastructure and high levels of government corruption. In 2006, protests pressured the government to hastily pass a new mining tax law that would require foreign companies to give up to 70% of profits on mineral resources, upon reaching a certain price level. This law has since been repealed by the current government.

Border Crossings

Zamyn-Uud (Mongolia)/Erenhot (China)
China and Mongolia share a 4,677 km border which stretches mostly along China's Inner Mongolia Autonomous Region and parts of Heilongjiang province.

The main crossing is between Zamyn Uud and Erenhot, on the Trans-Siberian Railway, which links Beijing and Moscow. There is also a highway which links Beijing and Hohhot, the capital of Inner Mongolia, but this is closed to two-way traffic. If open, it would potentially be a highway route to Ulan Ude, the capital of Buryat province in Russia and the third largest city in Siberia.

Rail is the preferred transportation method, however trains here have to be de-coupled and placed on different tracks at the border because Russian and Chinese tracks are different. This process can take up to 3 h. Trains run on a daily basis.

There are other road-based border crossings between Mongolia and China from Bulgan (Mongolia) and Qinghe (Xinjiang), Burgastay (Mongolia) and Loutoushitao (Xinjiang), Shiveehuren (Mongolia) and Sanzuoguli (Inner Mongolia), Gashuunsuhayt (Mongolia) and Ganjimod (Inner Mongolia). However, these routes are not usually open to foreign traffic, and many are close to sensitive military installations. Trying any of these routes is not recommended.

Borders may also be closed, including to rail traffic, during visits of the Dalai Lama to Mongolia and during heavy snow in the winter months.

Other seasonal border crossings between China and Mongolia exist on the Chinese side at Hongshanzui, Ulastay and Laoyemiao, all in northern Xinjiang and all connected to the Olgii Region of Mongolia. These are only open from May–October and can be prone to closure.

There are regular flights from Mongolia's capital of Ulaan Baatar to the Chinese cities of Beijing, Hohhot, Hailar and Tianjin.

Nepal

Formal name: Federal Democratic Republic of Nepal
Capital city: Kathmandu

GDP
US$35.81 billion

Total Imports & Exports
US$1.72 billion

World Bank
"Doing Business" Ranking
116 of 183

Population
29.39 million

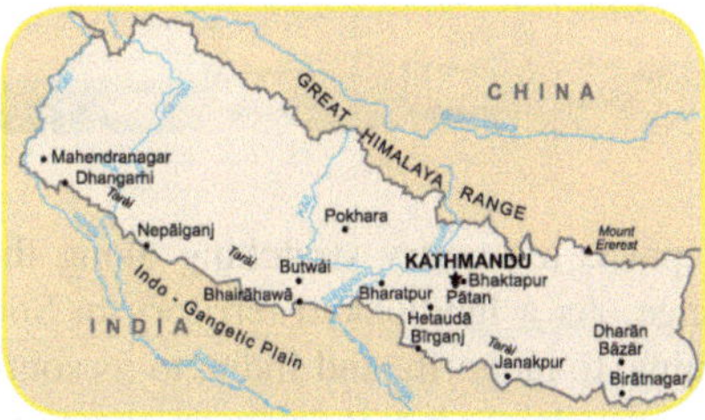

Nepal is bordered by China, Bangladesh and Bhutan. Nepal is not economically prosperous and political conflict has taken a strong grip over the country. Heavily reliant on foreign aid, Nepal is nonetheless a prime tourist destination, valued for its distinctive culture, beautiful scenery and the world's highest peak, Mount Everest. Nepal's currency is the rupee (NPR), which in 2010 traded at NPR72.56 to US $1. The most prevalent language spoken is Nepali.

Nepal became a republic in May 2008, ending the rule of a hereditary monarchy and a 10-year Maoist rebellion. In November 2007, a landmark peace deal was achieved and the Maoists joined an interim government. A new Maoist-dominated government took office in August 2008 before being toppled in May 2009 and replaced with a non-Maoist coalition. It is believed that Nepal will make the transition into a democracy although it is coming at the high cost of the country's present day peace and stability.

The Nepalese economy is not well developed and suffers from a severe lack of skilled labor, with a significant portion of the population living below the poverty line. Nepal's primary exports are clothing, textiles and jute goods. Primary export partners include India, the United States, Bangladesh and Germany.

The new budget for the 2011–2012 fiscal year was presented on July 15, 2011 and highlights include increases in public-sector salaries, a renewed focus on the development of the information technology sector, development of special economic zones and oil and gas industries.

Asia Briefing Ltd., *China's Neighbors*, China Briefing,
DOI: 10.1007/978-3-642-27615-6_10, © Asia Briefing Ltd. 2012

1 A Foothold in South Asia

Nepal is a country stretching along the spine of the great Himalayan mountain range. As a landlocked territory in South Asia, it acts as a buffer state between China, to its north, and India, to its south, east and west. Nepal is still a developing country, but what it lacks in economic riches, it makes up with its inspiring scenery and ancient culture.

Nepal is reputed to have the world's best hiking trails and eight of the world's ten highest mountain peaks are within its territory. The highest mountain in the world, Mount Everest, with a summit of 8,850 m (29,035 feet) above sea level, is located at its border with China.

The country is also important as the birthplace of Buddhism. Prince Siddhartha Gautama, known as the Buddha, was born in the sixth century B.C. in Lumbini, now a UNESCO World Heritage Site. Gautama was a young price who lived an extravagant sheltered life while his father, Suddhodana, was the ruler of the Sakya people. He began practicing asceticism and later went on to preach The Middle Way.

In 2010, an estimated 25% of the country's population lives below the poverty line. In the same year, per capita income was US $210.66. Agriculture contributes 33% to national GDP and is the livelihood for the majority of the population. This makes economic growth highly dependent on weather conditions. So it is no surprise that much of industrial activity involves the processing of agricultural products including jute, sugarcane, tobacco, and grain.

Prospects for major foreign investment will likely remain uncertain due to small market size, low levels of technology and isolated geographic location. Tourism, once a major source of foreign revenue, was an industry that was particularly hard-hit by political turmoil, and is only now regaining its strength.

The End of a Monarchy

Before becoming the Federal Democratic Republic of Nepal in 2008, the Shah dynasty had been ruling the country as a monarchy for 240 years. Royal members were not only seen as political leaders by Nepalese, but some also revered them as living incarnations of the Hindu god, Vishnu, the Preserver of Life. The monarchy was said to have given the country a sense of unity and a link between its past and present, fair play and freedom from petty political concerns.

However, the royal line was not infallible. When Nepal transitioned from an absolute to constitutional monarchy in 1990, many political parties rallied to gain control of the new parliament. Among these was the Communist Party of Nepal, which sought to turn the nation into a socialist state. While initially peaceful, many members of the Communist Party began to see the Nepalese royalty as a major hindrance to the country becoming a true people's republic, and strongly opposed to its continued status as head of the state. These tensions would boil to a civil war in 1996, when the Maoists, a revolutionary faction of the Communist Party, declared a protracted "People's War" against the monarchy.

In 2001, the monarchy was dealt its hardest blow. A drunken Crown Prince Dipendra would shock the nation by killing his parents, the King and Queen of Nepal, and seven other royals at a family party before committing suicide. Sources speculate that the prince's motive came from bitter arguments over his parent's disapproval of his choice of wife and plans to return to return the country to monarchial rule.

Several days following the tragedy, Gyanendra, one of the king's younger brothers, was crowned king. The tragedy was so scandalous, that many conspiracy theories spread. One popular theory pointed to Gyanendra as the mastermind of the massacre, for the obvious reason that he would be the one to benefit the most as the next in line to the throne.

For whatever reason, King Gyanendra's 7 year reign would prove futile, as he would always suffer under the shadow cast by the tragedy. His unpopularity would be cemented when he suspended the country's elected parliament in 2005, bringing the country back to autocratic rule. This action would eventually unite the Maoist rebels and the opposing political parties against the king.

The fighting between the rebel group and the government would only formally end in April 2008 when Nepal held national elections that saw the Maoists winning a majority of the constitutional assembly. The results reflected a nation that had grown jaded toward the monarchy and hoped for the dream of a better life offered by the Maoists. The Nepalese Civil War would finally end after more than 10 years of bloodshed that caused more that 17,000 deaths.

Following the Footsteps of Mao Zedong

From a group of guerillas terrorizing the countryside to a legitimate political party that would take 116 seats in the country's 601-member Constitutional Assembly, the Communist Party of Nepal-Maoisthas come a long way. The group was established by Pushpa Kamal Dahal, better known by his war name Prachanda, meaning "the fierce one."

The Maoists gained support from the poor Nepalese with their call for redistribution of land, extension of power centers into rural areas, elimination of the caste system, equal rights for women and the establishment of a republic.

In the past, Beijing has rejected links to the Nepalese Maoists saying that the movement has nothing todo with the late Chinese leader Mao Zedong, largely because the Nepalese cause has little resonance among contemporary Chinese leaders.

The country is currently in a state of flux. It remains to be seen if the Maoists can weather the complex political transition to shift their country from a feudal society to a modern, federal republic nation.

Despite recent developments the group is still included in the U.S. Terrorist Exclusion List and the Specially Designated Nationals and Blocked Persons List that bans them from any traveling or owning any property in the United States. However, there have been diplomatic efforts in 2011 to have the Maoists removed from the list.

In 2011, Nepal's Prime Minister Jhalanath Khanal resigned, reportedly because he was dissatisfied with his ability to achieve results. The country's President gave political parties an August 21, 2011 deadline to form a new government. It remains to be seen how successful the parties will be in reaching consensus, further threatening political stability.

Growing Ties to China

Prachanda's vocal stand for the country to be politically equidistant to both China and India caused worry in India. Historically, India and Nepal shared closer ties both in terms of culture and geography. Some even would go far as to say that Nepal serves as an informal "extension" of India, even though it maintains its sovereign jurisdiction.

India is currently Nepal's number one export and import market while China ranks as its second import market. The two countries have had strong military ties as India has long provided Nepal with training and equipment for its army. However, things may change as since 2008, the Maoists have sought to renegotiate the Indo-Nepal Treaty of Peace and Friendship that was first signed in 1950. The treaty had allowed the free movement of people and goods between the two nations including close collaboration on issues of defense and foreign affairs. However, some have criticized this treaty as an erosion of Nepalese sovereignty.

India has often used its influence with Nepal as a way to deflect its regional competitor, China. The nation lies at the foot of India's door and divides the two emerging economic giants from each other.

China may also want to increase its clout over Nepal so as not to encourage any more separatist movements coming from Tibet. Presently, around 20,000 Tibetan exiles live in Nepal.

In general, Chinese–Nepalese relations have been cordial, with stable political and economic relations. Recently, China has been working with Nepal to tap into its source of hydropower from the country's glacial lakes.

Border Crossings

Nepal shares a 1,400 km border with China (including Mount Everest) and has five open border passes. However, out of these crossings, only the China–Nepal highway is accessible by road and suitable for vehicles. It sits 3,750 m above sea level, the same altitude as the starting point and Tibetan capital Lhasa, and connects to Nepal's capital at Kathmandu. The road is also known as the Friendship Highway and was completed in 1966. It is a major route both for tourists and for trade between the two countries, and an important overland passage for goods travelling between India, Nepal and China.

Due to the high altitude and often severe weather conditions, there is no large-scale commercial development at the border, although sparse accommodations are available. Passageways through the border can be closed in winter due to severe weather, and were often closed during times of ethnic unrest in Tibet. There are plans to extend the existing China railway line to Lhasa west through Xigaze, and down to Kathmandu. If completed, this will directly link the Chinese, Nepalese and Indian national rail networks together and significantly boost the commercial viability of Lhasa and Kathmandu as trading hubs between India and China.

By air, there are regular, small-scale flights between Kathmandu and Lhasa.

North Korea

Formal name: Democratic People's Republic of Korea
Capital city: Pyongyang

GDP
US$28 billion

Total Imports & Exports
US$5.09 billion

World Bank "Doing Business" Ranking
N/A

Population
24.46 million

North Korea, or the "Hermit Kingdom," is one of the most closed off countries in the world. Bordered by China and splitting the Korean peninsula with South Korea, North Korea's geopolitical conflict has captured the attention of international media for the last decade. The country's currency is the won (KPW), which underwent a failed reform in 2009, damaging the country's economy and sparking resistance from local citizens. North Korea's official language is Korean.

North Korea emerged as a communist country in 1948, following the end of World War II. The country's founding ruler, Kim Il-sung, introduced the personal philosophy of Juche, or self-reliance, which has guided North Korea's development for the past 60 years. His son, Kim Jong-il, is currently the head of state but concerns over his health and diplomatic action by North Korean officials have prompted international suspicion that his son, Kim Jung-Un, will succeed him in the near future.

North Korea's pariah status in the world community, as well as its unwillingness to open to outsiders has made it difficult for the nation to receive substantial aid and assistance although it undoubtedly needs it. North Korea relies heavily on China, both for trade and for aid. The North Korean economy is estimated to have shrunken by 0.9% in 2009, although it has transitioned to focus in industry and services. The North Korean government has, however, committed to attracting foreign investment (subject to their terms and conditions) and has introduced a series of laws to facilitate this.

Asia Briefing Ltd., *China's Neighbors*, China Briefing,
DOI: 10.1007/978-3-642-27615-6_11, © Asia Briefing Ltd. 2012

1 Aid, Ideology, and Atomic Bombs

Kim Jong-Il's rule as leader of the Democratic People's Republic of Korea has been many things, but few can deny that he has remained true to the memory and vision of Kim Il-Sung, his father and the founding father of the DPRK. Nearly two decades after the death of Kim Il-Sung, the Hermit Kingdom remains one of the most secretive and rigid states in the world.

To its north, North Korea shares a 1,416 km border with China and a 19 km border with Russia. North and South Korea are buffered by a 238 km demilitarized zone.

One of the principles of North Korea's founding was that of "juche", or self-reliance, in both economic and political terms. Following a devastating famine in the 1990s and the enduring stagnation of the local economy, it has became clear that North Korea could no longer cut its economy off from the rest of the world. Some have characterized this shift in North Korean philosophy as "marketization without liberalization," with the leadership unwilling to compromise on their strict political ideology but slowly opening to foreign direct investment.

The state's elaborate propaganda machine feeds the cult of personality that surrounds Kim Jong-Il, portraying him as an incomparable leader continuing the country's revolutionary cause. Foreign media paints another picture of the leader, a bespectacled playboy with pompadour hair, a penchant for platform shoes and a liking for cognac, whose real scope of power is shrouded in mystery.

The nation's heavy-handed military focus has left the economy crippled and unable to handle modernization and natural disasters. Despite these obstacles, the state's objective in 2012, the hundredth anniversary of the birth of the nation's founding father Kim Il-sung, is to become a "strong and prosperous nation" focused on economic growth.

Kindred Spirit

North Korea finds its strongest ties with those that share its ideology: China, Vietnam, Laos, Cambodia, Burma and Russia. Of all its allies, China remains the DPRK's strongest economic and political ally. North Korea is heavily reliant on China for inputs like food, arms and fuel, and ties between the two countries have historically been close. In global political circles, China is often credited with having a large degree of control over North Korea although, according to Daniel Pinkston, a Northeast Asia expert at the International Crisis Group, "in general, Americans tend to overestimate the influence China has over North Korea."

Trade between North Korea and China amounted to US $2.79 billion in 2008, a 41.3% increase over 2007. According to the IMF, China has remained North Korea's primary trade partner since at least 1990.

China's interests in North Korea extend to national security, in the interest of managing peace along the border region which will insure China against a possible threat from democratic, and American-friendly, South Korea and Japan.

Going Nuclear

For all its economic woes, North Korea fancies itself as a nuclear and military power and claims to have the fifth largest army in the world.

The Six-Party Talks have been an ongoing series of diplomatic conventions, aiming to address North Korea's nuclear program development. Countries involved include China, the United States, North Korea, South Korea, Japan and Russia.

In 2002, North Korea admitted to having an active nuclear weapons program, which eventually led to the expulsion of international inspectors and international concern. By 2006, North Korea was at the receiving end of an international protest when it test-fired a long-range and medium-range missiles.

In 2007, the Six-Party Talks finally broke ground with North Korea agreeing to a deal that will give them aid and diplomatic concessions in exchange for completing the denuclearization process. However, talks broke down in April 2009 and North Korea began reversing efforts at disabling its nuclear facilities. It appeared that headway was being made in July 2011 after North Korea and the United States held "constructive" talks and indicated a desire to resume six-party talks.

A Question of Stability

Until the North Korea nuclear issue is resolved, the threat of nuclear weapons casts a shadow on the stability of East Asia. Tensions between the two Koreas are tense, with South Korea declaring North Korea its "principle enemy" under its most recent leadership. In 2010, the sinking of a South Korean naval ship and artillery fire at Yeonpyeong Island were both widely believed to be North Korean attacks on South Korea, and pushed relations between the two to a breaking point. North Korea's reluctance to give up its nuclear capability may force South Korea, Taiwan and Japan to also develop nuclear facilities.

While China has significant influence over North Korea, the country is still considered unstable. There has been hope, however, that North Korea will actively look at experimenting with the Chinese model of socialism and the development of a market economy. There have been signs before that North Korea might go down this path, Kim Jong-Il having previously visited free trade zones in Shenzhen.

Border Crossings

Sinuiju (North Korea)/Dandong (China)

Sited across the Yalu River and connected by the Sino-Korea Friendship Bridge, this border crossing is the most used and widely known between the two countries. Primarily existing as an access point for Chinese goods to enter North Korea, the route is heavily militarized but is accessible to commercial vehicles providing they have permits. Dandong has developed into a major trading center as a result and as a port, also supplies North Korea with products. Limited amounts of North Korean manufactured or finished goods also cross over here either via ship or road to markets in China and beyond.

Rajin (North Korea)/Hunchun (China)

Situated at the convergence of the borders of North Korea, China and Russia, 100 km southwest of Vladivostock, is a rail container goods-only transit point between Rajin, North Korea and Hunchun, China. It is close to the North Korean coast and 160 km from the major North Korean port of Cheongjin. Rajin is linked by rail to most major North Korean cities via the North Korean national rail network, while Hunchun is linked to the Russian rail network with direct access to the Russian port city of Posyet, Zarubino (63 km).

There are also border crossings between China and North Korea from the Chinese side at Ji'an, Linjiang, Changbai and Yanji, all in Jilin province. These are not open for tourism and are used mainly as government military and supply lines only.

Permits must be obtained in advance to travel to North Korea. These can be obtained either from the North Korean Embassy in Beijing, the North Korean Consulate in Hong Kong for business trips, or tourist trips can be arranged by Koryo Tours: www.koryogroup.com.

There are regular flights from Pyongyang to Beijing and Dalian.

Pakistan

Formal name: Islamic Republic of Pakistan
Capital city: Islamabad

GDP
US$464.9 billion

Total Imports & Exports
US$64.81 billion

World Bank "Doing Business" Ranking
83 of 183

Population
187.34 million

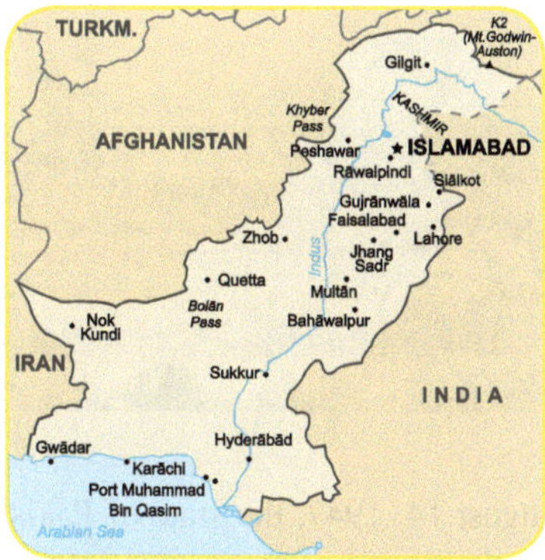

Pakistan was formed when India declared independence from British rule in 1947. Recurring conflict with India over Kashmir and other nationalistic issues have resulted in violence and social unrest. The country's currency is the Pakistani rupee (PKR), which in 2010 exchanged at PKR85.27 to US $1. There most common language spoken is Punjabi.

Pakistan is a federal republic, which was led by Pervez Musharraf through military rule from October 1999 until 2007. In 2008, Pakistan held parliamentary elections and elected Asif Ali Zardari as president in September of that year.

In 2011, inflation remained high in the country with an average consumer price inflation of 14%. Generally under-developed infrastructure in the country has prompted the government to seek public–private partnerships to help improve transportation routes.

Pakistan's export market is focused in textiles, rice, leather goods and carpets. GDP grew by 4.8% in 2010, while unemployment rose to a high of 15%. Pakistan's key export partners include the United States, the United Arab Emirates and Afghanistan. Comparatively, key import partners are China, and Saudi Arabia.

China and Pakistan celebrated the 60th anniversary of diplomatic relations in 2011. China has long been a supporter of Pakistan's nuclear development program and is an important ally as China looks for new land routes to international markets.

Asia Briefing Ltd., *China's Neighbors,* China Briefing,
DOI: 10.1007/978-3-642-27615-6_12, © Asia Briefing Ltd. 2012

1 An Enduring Alliance

On August 14, 1947, the state of Pakistan was born. The Indian subcontinent was effectively ripped at the seams into a Muslim East Pakistan and a Hindu West Bengal after 89 years under the British Raj.

National assets like the British Indian Army, the Indian Civil Service, railways, central treasury and other administrative services had to be divided accordingly. The separation proved chaotic and came so suddenly that many people found themselves living on the wrong side of the partition.

Muslims, Sikhs and Hindus were forced to move out, leading to riots that killed an estimated half a million people and rendered millions homeless. During the process, the regions of Jammu and Kashmir remained undecided on which side to join. The issue still remains contested today and is one of the currents running deep in the rivalry between India and Pakistan.

Pakistan has laid claims on Jammu and Kashmir because a majority of their population is Muslim while India maintains the claim over the regions based on an October 1947 instrument of accession that shows the Maharaja agreed to join India.

The Kashmir issue would lead India and Pakistan to war in 1947 and 1965. In 1971, another war erupted when India supported the Bengalis, which led East Pakistan to become present day Bangladesh. Violence would again come in 1989, when an armed Islamic resistance emerged against Indian rule in the Kashmir valley, with some wanting independence while others calling for accession with Pakistan.

Bitter Rivals

In the 61 years after partition, stability remains an elusive dream for Pakistan. The country stands on unstable ground in both its internal and international affairs.

It attempted to defuse tensions with India in 1997 but talks only led to a stalemate. Driven by the fear of war, India and Pakistan aggressively worked to stock their nuclear arsenals during the 1990s. This resulted in sanctions from both the U.N. and the rest of the international community.

In May 1999, India launched air strikes against Pakistani-supported militants found in the Indian administered area of Kashmir. The fighting would displace an estimated 50,000 people from their homes. In the same year, General Musharraf would head a military coup in the country that overthrew Prime Minister Nawaz Sharif.

Tensions between India and Pakistan would regularly reignite through the years. In 1998, Pakistan and India would court nuclear confrontation. India detonated underground nuclear tests in Rajasthan near the border with Pakistan. Pakistan countered by conducting six tests in Baluchistan.

In 2001, the United States became a major player in the region after the 9/11 attacks. It would forge an alliance with Pakistan based on security interests and its shared 2,430 km border with Afghanistan.

Currently, Pakistan's economy is in tatters, while the Taliban insurgency from neighboring Afghanistan has escalated. This has been further exacerbated by cooling relations with the United States. Its political realm is in similar shape, with a history filled with violence, corruption and scandal.

One of the most shocking issues in recent times was the death of Benazir Bhutto in December 2007. She was then the popular opposition leader and had previously served as the country's premier twice from 1988 to 1990 and 1993 to 1996. Shortly after returning from exile, Bhutto was killed in a political rally when an assassin first shot her before taking her own life in a suicide blast.

Pervez Musharraf, the president of Pakistan at the time, would face unpopular perceptions as well as deepening scrutiny over his suspected role in the attacks. This would ultimately lead to his resignation in August 2008. On September 2008, Pakistan People's Party leader and Benazir Bhutto's widower, Asif Ali Zardari, was elected as Pakistan's new president and remains in this role today.

On May 1, 2011, American forces launched a military operation in Abbottabad, Pakistan, which killed Osama bin Laden, the Al-Qaeda leader and one of the key architects of the 9/11 attacks. While Pakistan is one of the United States' most important allies in the War on Terror, bin Laden's death was nevertheless a serious blow to US-Pakistan relations, as American officials began to doubt the competency of Pakistan's military intelligence, especially since the Al-Qaeda leader was found hiding in compound near a Pakistani military academy.

Citing "difficulties" in the two countries' relationship," the United States suspended approximately US $800 million in annual military aid that was to be given to Pakistan in July 2011. This represented more than a third of the US $2 billion that is often sent to the country's armed forces.

Comrades-in-Arms

During all this turmoil, China would remain Pakistan's constant ally by supplying military arms, equipment and vehicles. Much of this relationship has been supported by strategic and geographic interests.

China's support of Pakistan is an indirect way of containing India. "Traditionally, the driving factor for China was a hedge against India, and for Pakistan it was gaining access to civilian and military resources," Kenneth Lieberthal, a China expert and professor at the University of Michigan told the Council of Foreign Relations.

Oil is the driving force of the world's most powerful economies, and China's aggressive pursuit of it may be an additional motive for its deepening relationship with Pakistan. China has long been helping to build the Gwadar Port in Pakistan, which is strategically located in the mouth of the Straits of Hormuz. In May 2011, the two countries agreed that China will be given control of the port, giving the country access to the Western regions of the Indian Ocean.

China's access to the area will secure its oil supplies shipped from the Persian Gulf in anticipation of ballooning gas needs in the next decade. Currently, around 80% of China-bound oil and liquid natural gas passes through the Indian Ocean. Docks such as the Gwadar Port will give China access to the northern sections of the ocean, and allow the country to better secure its sea routes.

China will also be able to access Iranian oil through Pakistan via a pipeline running through the Karakoram Highway. The highway begins at China's Xinjiang running through the northern areas of Pakistan. The pipeline should serve as a complement to China's oil deals with Russia and Myanmar.

This is where China clashes with India. India also has escalating energy needs as its economy develops and it will be scrambling against China for control over the same oil resources in the region. Currently, India has a strong military presence in the Andaman and Nicobar Islands in the Bay of Bengal, a key area at the northeastern regions of the Indian Ocean. This position gives India the opportunity to compromise Chinese energy imports if the need arises, but the inverse is also true. China's relationships with Pakistan and Myanmar have allowed it to invest in a military presence within India's backyard.

In 2011, China and Pakistan celebrated 60 years of cooperation since the formal establishment of diplomatic relations in 1951. Under the Free Trade Agreement between the two countries, bilateral trade between China and Pakistan has increased from US $3 billion in 2005, to US $8.7 billion in 2010. Both countries are now in talks to increase the trade volume to US $15 billion within the next 2 years.

Border Crossings

Gilgit (Pakistan)/Kashgar (China)
There is a border crossing at Suster Port in Pakistan, extending across a 125 km long demilitarized zone which stretches north along the Pamir valley to Khunjerab Port, Taxkorgan, an ethnic Kazak town in China's far west corner. It is only open from May 1 to November 30, due to the severe winter weather conditions and has an average elevation of 4,000 m.

Khunjerab Port is 270 km from Gilgit, the regional capital of northern Pakistan, and 870 km from Islamabad, the capital. On the Chinese side, it is 420 km from Kashgar and 1,890 km from Urumqi. It is the only overland border crossing between the countries and is the route of the fabled Karakoram Highway, being an ancient part of the Southern Silk Road. Marco Polo was said to have travelled this way and to have stayed at Taxkorgan's Fort, an ancient caravan stop over and trading center—the ruins of which still stand impressive today.

Feasibility studies are currently being carried out to assess the viability of extending both the Pakistani rail network from Peshawar to Gilgit, and the Chinese network south from Kashgar (currently its most western point) and for them to interlink. Doing so will lead to increased prosperity within the region, which is close to the troubled tribal areas of North Pakistan and Afghanistan, as well as enable both countries to share and develop more trade.

There are regular flights from Islamabad to Kashgar and Urumqi.

from US $4 billion in 2009, to US $8.7 billion in 2010. Both countries are now in talks to increase the trade volume to US $15 billion within the next 2 years.

Border Crossings

Gilgit (Pakistan)/Kashgar (China)

There is a border crossing at Sost. Part in Pakistan, extending across a 135 km long demilitarized zone which stretches north along the Pamir valley to Khunjerab into Taxkorgan, an ethnic Tajik town in China's far west region. It is only open from May 1 to November 30 due to the severe winter weather conditions and has an average elevation of 4,700 m.

Khunjerab Pass is 270 km from Gilgit, the regional capital of northern Pakistan, and 870 km from Islamabad, the capital. On the Chinese side, it is 420 km from Kashgar and 1,470 km from Urumqi. It is the only overland border crossing between the countries and is the route of the fabled Karakoram Highway, being an ancient part of the Southern Silk Road. Marco Polo was said to have travelled this way and to have stayed at Taxkorgan's Fort, an ancient caravan stop over and trading center, the ruins of which still stand impressively today.

Feasibility studies are currently being carried out to assess the viability of extending the Pakistani rail network from Peshawar to Gilgit, and the Chinese network south from Kashgar. Currently, the most western point one can reach by train is Kashgar. This would lead to increased prosperity within the region, which is close to the troubled tribal areas of North Pakistan and Afghanistan, as well as enable both countries to share and develop more trade.

There are regular flights from Islamabad to Kashgar and Urumqi.

Russia

Formal name: Russian Federation
Capital city: Moscow

GDP
US$2.22 trillion

Total Imports & Exports
US$619.63 billion

World Bank
"Doing Business" Ranking
123 of 183

Population
138.74 million

Russia is physically the largest country in the world, and hidden within its vast landscape are valuable oil and gas resources. The country's currency is the Russian ruble (RUB) which traded at RUB30 to US $1 in 2010. Russia has a rich literary history, and the official language spoken is Russian although there are a large number of minority languages.

Dmitry Medvedev has served as the country's president since 2008, succeeding Vladimir Putin. Putin today serves as Prime Minister and retains considerable influence.

Tension in the Caucasus region of Chechnya has plagued the country for more than a decade. Violence has drawn the attention of human rights groups, both local and foreign, as allegations of human rights abuses have come against the state. A major suicide bomb in September of 2010 called into question the stability of the region, once again.

The 2008 global financial slow down affected Russia deeply, seeing the collapse of the stock market in mid-September 2008, as investor confidence fell and capital flooded out of the country. Falling commodity prices hit the country's substantial oil and gas sector, stalling economic growth.

The nation's economic outlook brightened in 2010, following the implementation of a number of government policies and an improvement in the global marketplace. In retrospect, Moscow has begun to push for the diversification of the economy away from reliance on commodities in the direction of innovation and diversification.

Asia Briefing Ltd., *China's Neighbors,* China Briefing,
DOI: 10.1007/978-3-642-27615-6_13, © Asia Briefing Ltd. 2012

1 Partners and Competitors

The Russian Federation is a unique nation with one foot in the east and the other in the west. The country physically spans the planet starting from northern Asia and covers about 40% of Europe. Russia's beginnings can be traced back to as early as the third century when the East Slavs were ruled by the seafaring Vikings. Since then, the centuries have come and gone and have left behind a history rich with culture, science and ideology.

Russia has abundant stores of raw materials and is a world leader in the production of natural gas and oil, of which it is estimated to produce almost a quarter of the world's total production. Its other main exports include wood and wood products, metals, chemicals, weapons and military equipment.

By the end of the Cold War and the disintegration of Soviet Union in 1991, Russia was left to deal with the problems of a collapsing economy, aging military infrastructure (including huge nuclear weapon stores), rampant corruption and eroding clout as its western neighbors looked towards Europe for direction and support.

Under the contemporary presidency of Vladimir Putin, Russia would regain its confidence and begin improving its economy. According to his predecessor Boris Yeltsin, Mr. Putin was a man who could "unite around himself those who will revive Great Russia." After winning two terms as president, he now acts as prime minister.

Clash of the Titans

Over the years, Chinese and Russian relations have walked the tightrope between friendship and war. Despite sharing similar ideologies and a common perceived Imperialist enemy, the United States, the two often do not see eye-to-eye.

During the Cold War in the 1960s, relations were strained over ideological and eventually, border issues. China wanted to step out of the former Soviet Union's shadow to claim leadership in the Communist movement. It was only in 1976 that Chinese–Soviet relations normalized, only to be disrupted when China briefly invaded Vietnam in 1978. In 2004, a long-disputed border issue was resolved when Russia agreed to cede Yinlong Island and half of Heixiazi Island to China.

Another prickly territory issue is Russia's large port city of Vladivostok, located near the Chinese–Russian border and North Korea. The region is unique because of its population of Russians, Chinese and Korean living side by side. Sources report that prior to Russia's acquisition of the city, through the Treaty of Aigun in 1858, it was first occupied by the Manchu people. In its historical atlases, Beijing has not been shy in claiming that Vladivostok once belonged to China.

Trade and Energy

Chinese–Russian relations were shaped by the Treaty of Good–Neighborliness and Friendly Cooperation, formalized in 2001. The treaty outlined plans for the next 20 years that include peaceful relations, economic cooperation, geopolitical reliance and a defense pact to increase military cooperation. The treaty allows for a cooperative approach to environmental technology regulations, energy conservation, and international finance and trade. As well, Russia also agreed that Taiwan was "an inalienable part of China."

Since then, Chinese–Russian relations have engaged with topics such as energy development, spaceflight and aviation, nuclear power, mechanics and the high-tech industry.

Trade between China and Russia in machinery and electronics is expected to reach US $30 billion, roughly a third of total anticipated trade volume of US $100 billion, by 2015. In 2010, bilateral trade increased by nearly 50% from 2009 to reach US $57.1 billion, with the majority of growth attributable to Chinese exports.

In 2006, China and Russia were in talks to develop a pipeline to transport natural gas from western Siberia into eastern China. By 2010, however, an inability to come to an agreement on prices stalled talks and global geopolitical events aggravated the circumstances. Unrest in the Middle East and increased demand for natural gas by Japan (because of the 2011 earthquake) has put upward pressure on prices, which China is resisting. As of now, the future of this project remains unclear, although as China decreases its dependence on coal, negotiations may take on a new meaning.

Another pipeline with a capacity of 38 billion cubic meters per year is also set to connect eastern Siberia and Sakhalin Island to China's Heilongjiang province by 2016.

Russia is angling itself to become the main supplier of oil for its energy-strapped Asian neighbors by developing a 4,000 km oil pipeline, starting from eastern Siberia and stretching to Kozimo Bay in the nearby Sea of Japan. The project's Phase 1 will give China a spur pipeline that promises to deliver up to 300,000 barrels of oil daily.

State-run Gazprom is the world's largest producer of natural gas and supplies nearly a quarter of Europe's natural gas. The company was hard hit by the global financial crisis, with European demand falling. By 2011, the outlook began to brighten and the company was reporting output was expected to reach pre-2009 levels by 2013. Furthermore, Gazprom has begun to investigate new oil fields in remote regions of Russia as older sources are showing declining output. Gazprom's natural gas is transported through the Unified Gas Supply System, the world's largest gas transmission system, with its more than 160,000 km of trunk lines and branches.

Russia's monopolistic ambitions in gas have already attracted challengers. Turkmenistan has signed a deal with China for a gas pipeline called the Central Asia Gas Pipeline that will annually deliver 30 billion cubic meters of gas for 30 years. The gas field is located by the Amudarya River and will partially minimize dependence on Russian energy.

A Race to the Finish

Beneath the froth of diplomatic talk, there is a silent economic storm brewing between Russia and China as they race for domination in Central Asia. Federico Bordonaro, a Rome-based analyst, told Radio Free Europe "In the medium term, competition between China and Russia is set to take a more important place in relations between Beijing and Moscow. This is due to the fact that Beijing absolutely needs energy and the same energy is in the strategic interests of Russia."

China and Russia are both eyeing the reserves of their Central Asian neighbors, particularly oil from Kazakhstan and natural gas from Turkmenistan. Russia has made the move to guard its cash cow by regulating the flow of Turkmen gas through its series of pipelines.

According to Radio Free Europe, Fyodor Lukyanov, editor in chief of a Moscow journal, said "We will see a soft competition that could heat up as China becomes more successful. Russia doesn't want to be China's junior partner in this region."

Border Crossings

Russia and China share a 4,200-km-long border, whose definitions were only settled in 1991 with a further minor amendment in 2004. Much of the border remains militarized and is difficult to cross as it follows the length of the Amur River.

Blagoveshchensk (Russia)/Heihe (China)
These two towns have formed a free trade zone with visa free passage across each side (restricted to the city limits) for inhabitants. They are situated across from each other on the banks of the Amur River about 110 km south of the trans-Siberian railway, some 500 km directly north of Harbin. The combined population of the cities is about 500,000 and are major hubs of Russian-Sino trade. Cross-border trade is carried out by boat in the summer, and by hovercraft and bus in winter when the river freezes. It is not possible to cross the border here without pre-obtained visas.

Zabaykalsk (Russia)/Manzhouli (China)
This is the largest border and trade crossing point between Russia and China and accounts for some 60% of all import/export volumes between China, Russia and Eastern Europe. It is the single largest land border crossing by volume of people and goods in China. The crossing is additionally connected to the Chinese Highway 226 from Harbin to the south east, and on the Russian side to Highway 121 to Chita, a major Russian trading city, some 350 km due north–east. This border crossing is also a terminus for the main Beijing–Moscow rail line, while the infrastructure on both sides provides for extensive warehousing and repacking services.

Both Chita and Manzhouli have airports connecting them with respective major domestic destinations. Manzhouli is to open a Shangri-La Hotel in 2009.

Pogranichny (Russia)/Suifenhe (China)
This crossing, also known as Grodekovo on the Russian side, lies just 40 km east of Mudanjiang on the eastern border of China's Heilongjiang province, some 140 km north of the key Russian port of Vladivostock. This crossing is connected to Vladivostock by highway and rail.

Mudanjiang also serves as a road and rail hub for goods coming to and from the regional Chinese cities of Changchun, its largest auto manufacturing base, Harbin, the provincial capital, and Hunchen, on the border with North Korea, and continues these links directly to this border.

Tajikistan

Formal name: Republic of Tajikistan
Capital city: Dushanbe

GDP
US$5.64 billion

Total Imports & Exports
US$5.02 billion

World Bank "Doing Business" Ranking
139 of 183

Population
7.63 million

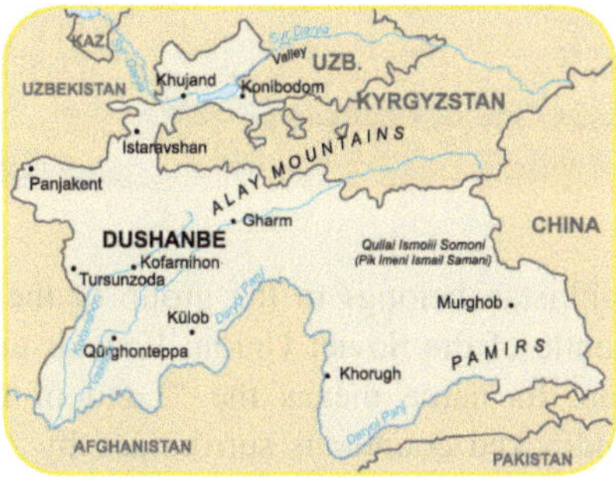

Tajikistan is an impoverished nation, bordered and culturally influenced by Kyrgyzstan, Uzbekistan and Afghanistan. Declaring independence from the Soviet Union in 1991, the country suffered through a 5-year civil war ending in 1997. With its under-developed economy, a large number of Tajiks look to neighboring countries for employment. The country's official language is Tajik, although Russian is commonly used in business and governmental transactions. The Tajikistani somoni (TJS) traded at TJS4.3788 to US $1 in 2010.

Tajikistan's key export commodities are aluminum, electricity and cotton and its largest trading partner by volume is China. Comparatively, Tajikistan is heavily reliant on imports for petroleum products and its major import partner is Russia. Russia has substantial influence in the country and aside from economic aid, also plays an important role in Tajikistan's border security.

Tajikistan's president is Emomali Sharipovich Rakhmon, who has governed for more than a decade. The country's legislative practices are not transparent and the most recent elections have not met international democratic standards.

Tajikistan has expanding diplomatic relations with China and Tajikistan's Labor Migration Service registered nearly 82,000 Chinese workers in Tajikistan in 2010, a more than 25-fold increase from 2006.

China has aided in the construction of roads and tunnels between the two countries. A 130-year old border dispute between Tajikistan and China was resolved in 2011, with Tajikistan ceding 1,142 km^2 of land to China.

Asia Briefing Ltd., *China's Neighbors,* China Briefing,
DOI: 10.1007/978-3-642-27615-6_14, © Asia Briefing Ltd. 2012

1 Investing in Stability

Tajikistan belongs to the group of the Central Asian 'stans' formerly under the mantle of the Soviet Union: Kazakhstan, Kyrgyzstan, Turkmenistan and Uzbekistan. Its name means the "Land of the Tajiks" in Persian. The mountainous landlocked country is surrounded by Afghanistan to its south, Uzbekistan to the west, Kyrgyzstan to the north, and China to the east.

Central Asia sits on some of the largest untapped energy reserves in the world although it is still plagued by poverty, corruption, despotic regimes and economic instability. This heady combination makes for a fertile breeding ground for Islamic militarism, exported from neighboring Afghanistan.

Often Central Asia's problems do not prominently figure in global consciousness, although its geographic significance has not gone unnoticed by Western leaders—it is a vital part of the Muslim world. But more than anything, the region is a site for Islamic solidarity due to ethnic affinity and geographic proximity with regional players like Iran, Afghanistan and Pakistan. It is a volatile region that sees the flow of drugs, arms and Islamic militarism through its porous borders. Estimates show that almost 90% of heroin smuggled to the West come from Central Asia.

Geography is Destiny

Of all the Central Asian states, Tajikistan is the poorest and the most fragile. It is not rich in oil like Kazakhstan or Uzbekistan and has never quite recovered from its former Soviet Union days. The government has been unable to escape flawed structural reforms, corruption, bad governance, unemployment, power shortages, and external debt.

Tajikistan relies on exports of cotton and aluminum to support the economy. As well, sources point out that, other than hydroelectric power, Tajikistan does not offer much in terms of natural resources.

In January 2007, China agreed to loan Tajikistan US $200 million for a period of 25 years at 1% interest to build the Zeravshan Hydroelectric plant Upon completion, the hydroelectric power plant is expected to have an annual output of around 600 million kilowatts.

There are reports that the country has large coal reserves, but its mining industry has remained undeveloped since 1991. Tajikistan has not produced any coal despite having 29 coalfields with an estimated value of more than 15.3 billion tons, or roughly 41% of Central Asia's reserves.

The Afghanistan Factor

One of the most pressing issues at the moment is Tajikistan's shared border with Afghanistan, a source of Islamic extremism and illegal drug trafficking. In geopolitical terms, Tajikistan offers a way to maneuver with or against Afghanistan. The United States knows this and in 2010, increased aid to Tajikistan by more than 11% to US $58.65 million.

During the years prior to the fall of the Soviet Union, Afghan mujahideen groups built an Islamic military in Tajikistan with the help of Pakistan's Inter-Services Intelligence. As well, 150 Afghan groups were set up along the Tajik border, complete with training centers for youth, with the goal of flushing out Communism and installing Islamic governance.

Ensuring the Future

China knows relations in Central Asia are key and it can be assumed that China's ambitions for its Tajikistan relations will fulfill two things: first, a way to stabilize a mercurial Central Asia and second, to contain any separatist movements in its Xinjiang Uygur Autonomous Region.

"China's policy aims for a peaceful external environment conducive to curb secessionism and extremism in Xinjiang, besides securing China's national security and economic objectives," said Dr. K. Warikoo, the Director of Central Asian Studies Program at Jawaharlal Nehru University.

Already, China has engaged in discussions with Tajikistan through the Shanghai Cooperation Organization (SCO) and through the framework of the SCO, China and Tajikistan have promised to improve bilateral trade relations and cooperation against terrorism, separatism and extremism.

Both China and Tajikistan often hold joint military exercises. In 2011, China, Kyrgyzstan and Tajikistan collectively participated in an anti-terror drill in China's far west Xinjang Uygur Autonomous Region.

Since the establishment of Chinese and Tajikistani formal relations 15 years ago, the two countries have signed more than 105 agreements and in 2010, bilateral trade grew to US $1.4 billion.

Xinjiang, a name meaning "new territory" in Mandarin, was declared a Chinese province by the Chinese Communists in 1949. By 1955, it was classified as an autonomous region. Its 20 million residents are made up of mostly Muslim Turkic groups, the largest of which are the Uighurs, who have closer cultural ties to Central Asian countries than to the local Han Chinese.

There is fear that a resurgence in Afghan radical Islamic activity, crossing from Tajikistan, could embolden Uyghur separatism in Xinjiang and lead to an unstable border area in western China.

Border Crossings

Murgab (Tajikistan)/Kulma Karosy (China)

The Kalasu Port serving this border is still relatively small, lying at an altitude of 3,500 m. With Chinese assistance, the road, and the 500 km border between the two countries has provided greater security against human trafficking and narcotics. This road has also assisted with a continuing resurgence of overland trade between these two countries, helping to lift Tajikistan out of poverty and reestablishing Murgab as a Silk Road trading center.

Vietnam

Formal name: Socialist Republic of Vietnam
Capital city: Hanoi

GDP
US$103.6 billion

Total Imports & Exports
US$167.6 billion

World Bank
"Doing Business" Ranking
78 of 183

Population
90.55 million

Vietnam is located to the south of China and is bordered by Laos and Cambodia. A rapidly developing country, Vietnam aspires to become a developed nation by 2020. Vietnam declared independence on September 2, 1945, ending years of conflict with France and fighting between northern and southern Vietnam. Vietnam's currency is the dong (VND), which traded at VND19,148.9 to US $1 in 2010. The official language spoken is Vietnamese. Vietnam's president, Nguyen Minh Triet, attained the country's highest position in 2006 and was reconfirmed in January of 2011.

In the late 1980s, Vietnam opened its economy to global markets and foreign investment through implementing economic reforms. Since then, Vietnam's economy has posted strong growth, at a peak of roughly 8% of GDP year-on-year in the 1990s but slowing in 2010 to 6.78% in 2009.

In 2010, utilized foreign direct investment totaled US $11 billion, a 10% increase over 2009. Vietnam's key exports are clothing, shoes, rice and machinery and key export partners are the United States, Japan and China. In fact, Vietnam's development in agricultural production since the opening of its economy has raised Vietnam as the world's second-largest exporter of rice.

Relations with China have taken a negative hit in the last year over repeated disputes in the South China Sea. In September, 2010 Vietnamese and Chinese officials committed to infrastructure development of links between the two countries to facilitate trade.

Asia Briefing Ltd., *China's Neighbors,* China Briefing,
DOI: 10.1007/978-3-642-27615-6_15, © Asia Briefing Ltd. 2012

1 Paving the Way for Development

Nearly 30 years ago, Dang Dong sat in the center of an advancing Chinese army. Infuriated by Vietnam's invasion of neighboring Cambodia, China initiated a short and bloody incursion into northern Vietnam. By the time Chinese tanks had retreated, much of the provinces of Cao Bang, Lao Cai and Lang Song were in ruins. Today the two nations consider Dang Dong vital to their economic development, and the countries are now looking at new roads and transportation agreements to not only bring new prosperity to the region, but also to further solidify a once icy relationship.

In 2005, then-Vietnamese President Tran Duc Luong and Chinese President Hu Jintao issued a joint communiqué recognizing their common goals for expanding bilateral relations and addressing territorial border issues. The agreement set the ball rolling on a 5-year plan that aims to lead to US $15 billion two way trade by 2010 under the banner, "two corridors, and one economic belt."

By 2011, that objective had been met above and beyond original expectations. Bilateral trade had grown to the extent that China held the title of Vietnam's largest trading partner for the previous 6 years and bilateral trade turnover totaled US $30 billion in 2010.

For at least the last decade, discussions between the Asia Development Bank and key Asian countries have focused on the development of economic corridors to improve relations. The Kunming-Laocai-Hanoi- Haiphong corridor, or the North South Economic Corridor, will connect inland China with coastal Vietnam.

In 2007, the Asia Development Bank announced it would be financing a US $1.1 billion project to build a highway to connect Hanoi, Vietnam with cities in China's Yunan province. The highway—designated Asian Highway 14 in Vietnam—will link up across the border with one that is already under construction on the Chinese side, and when completed, give access for Chinese goods in Southern China to the Vietnamese port of Haiphong and increased markets in southern and central China to Vietnamese exporters.

The Guangxi Zhuang Autonomous Region borders Vietnam and is nestled between the provinces of Yunnan, Guizhou, Hunan and Guangdong. Guangxi is a key foreign-trade center for China and a key gateway to ASEAN nations, which is an integral trading partner and export market for China. Two-way trade between Guangxi and Vietnam, Guangxi's largest trading partner, totaled more than US $4 billion in 2009.

In 2010, the United States remained Vietnam's top export market, with an estimated export turnover of US $12.8 billion, a 25.4% increase over the previous year. The European Union ranked second in terms of export volume at US $10 billion, while trade with ASEAN totaled US $9.3 billion.

As of April 2011, foreign investors registered to invest US $4.024 billion in Vietnam, representing a more than 50% increase over the same period in 2009. Singapore ranked first, as the largest source of FDI, followed by Hong Kong. China ranked 15th with 24 projects worth more than US $29 million. The two have also participated in exchanging human resource skills that resulted in China training 1,357 officials and technical personnel along with lending expertise for electric power station, light rail, communication, and mining industry projects.

History

China and Vietnam share a history that goes beyond a common 16,430-km land border and shared use of the Gulf of Tonkin. During the first century B.C., China's Han Dynasty ruled the Red River Delta in northern Vietnam. Chinese rule brought the development of infrastructure and agriculture for the Vietnamese, along with the imposition of Chinese culture. Although Chinese language, customs and political institutions were mandated requirements, Nam Viet, as it was formerly called, never fully embraced Chinese culture. By the tenth century, the Vietnamese were able to pry loose from Chinese rule.

In 1974, Sino-Vietnamese relations were aggravated when China troops grabbed the western part of the much-disputed Paracel Islands occupied by a South Vietnamese garrison. Trade relations between the two continued to sour before halting altogether in 1979 when China launched a 29 day military campaign on Vietnam's border. China reasoned that the move was in response to Vietnam's invasion of Cambodia and its alliance with the Soviet Union. It was only in 1991 that relations between the two started to defrost, bringing about accelerated bilateral trade.

Feeding the Dragon

China is the leading manufacturer and user of coal in the world. Coal is the force that fuels China's boom and answers a majority of its energy needs.

Xu Dingming, one of the people tasked to manage China's energy policy, has said in the past that coal answers the country's urgent need for more power. Even with China's sprinting growth, more than 10 million of its citizens still have no access to electricity.

In the next decade alone, China is expected to construct up to 500 coal-fired power plants to accommodate increasing energy needs. Certainly, within the last 5 years China has overtaken the United States as the world's largest emitters of carbon dioxide and the country's leadership has been increasingly turning its attention to China's high levels of pollution.

So where does Vietnam figure into all of this? Besides being a geographically ideal trading partner, Vietnam is also the largest exporter of anthracite coal in the world and its coal reserves, the majority of which are anthracite, are estimated at 150 million tons. Anthracite coal is considered the best of its kind because it burns at high temperatures, is almost smokeless and is utilized to make high-grade steel.

By mid-2011, China was importing roughly 143 million tons of coal and Vietnam was supplying more than 70% of its total coal exports to China.

Crude oil is another top Vietnamese export to China and the rest of the world. Vietnam is the third biggest crude oil exporter in Southeast Asia. Vietnam does not have major refining facilities and only opened its first oil refinery in 2009. The majority of what the country produces is exported, and Vietnam relies heavily on imported petroleum products to meet domestic needs.

What Lies Ahead

The China–Vietnam relationship is not without its flaws, especially for lesser-developed Vietnam. Although two-way trade has hiked up in the past years by as much as 40% annually, both countries stand on uneven ground with China seemingly getting more perks out of the relationship. For one, China enjoyed a US $12.7 billion trade surplus with Vietnam in 2010. While China is one of Vietnam's largest trade partners, trade with Vietnam only counts for less than 6% of China's total export trade. The discrepancy can be traced mainly to the type of products Vietnam exports to China: coal, crude oil, rubber, foodstuff, seafood, footwear to name a few. The majority are either raw materials or low-valueadded manufactured goods.

On the other end of the spectrum, China's top exports to Vietnam include high-value-added manufactured goods like cars, motorbike parts, machinery, package equipment, pharmaceuticals, and petroleum.

An intensified trade relationship with China will require Vietnam to step up its efforts to come into its own and step out of China's shadow. Ultimately, Vietnam needs to open its borders to trade but also upgrade its manufacturing sector or risk becoming an assembly factory and producer of raw materials for China.

Border Crossings

Vietnam has well developed border crossings with China and there are several key crossing points.

Dong Dang (Vietnam)/Pingxiang (China)
This is the most developed border crossing between Vietnam and China, and is developing into a significant trading hub. Several highway crossings and a main rail line all pass through this point. Pingxiang, on the Chinese side, is a city of 2.5 million. There is an economic and trade development zone in Pingxiang. This crossing marks the route of rail traffic directly between Hanoi and northeast to Nanning, the capital of Guangxi, a distance of 400 km.

Lao Cai (Vietnam)/Hekou (China)
This is also a major crossing, with road and rail connections here running northwest between Hanoi and Kunming, the capital of Yunnan province, a total distance of 490 km.

There are also pedestrian and tourist crossings between Mong Cai on the East Vietnamese coast and Dongxing in Guangxi, and another eleven land crossings along the north Vietnamese border with Guangxi autonomous region and Yunnan province. However these are not always open for foreign travelers.

There are regular flights from Hanoi to Kunming, Nanning and Guangzhou.

MIX
Papier aus verantwortungsvollen Quellen
Paper from responsible sources
FSC® C105338

If you have any concerns about our products,
you can contact us on
ProductSafety@springernature.com

In case Publisher is established outside the EU,
the EU authorized representative is:
Springer Nature Customer Service Center GmbH
Europaplatz 3, 69115 Heidelberg, Germany

Printed by Libri Plureos GmbH
in Hamburg, Germany